Entwined
Celtic Cables Collection
by Knit Picks

Copyright 2020 © Knit Picks

All rights reserved. This book or any portion thereof may not be reproduced or used in any manner whatsoever without the express written permission of the publisher except for the use of brief quotations in a book review.

Photography by John Cranford

Printed in the United States of America
First Printing, 2020
ISBN 978-1-62767-255-9
Versa Press, Inc.
800-447-7829
www.versapress.com

CONTENTS

Big Pretzel Coat *by Adrienne Larsen* — 6

Chalkney Cardigan *by Claire Slade* — 16

Cluthar Hat *by Joan Beck* — 26

Coppice Mitts *by Claire Slade* — 32

Kells Wrap *by Allison Griffith* — 38

Knots & Chains Pullover *by Sandi Rosner* — 44

Lindisfarne Poncho *by Bridget Pupillo* — 50

Morag Pullover *by Elly Doyle* — 60

Nevern Throw *by Kath Andrews* — 70

Nuallan Cape & Capelet *by Jen Pierce* — 82

Parting of the Ways Pullover *by Theresa Shingler* — 92

Sennit Vest *by Margaret Mills* — 100

Sonja's Hat *by Hope Vickman* — 108

Glossary — 118

CHALKNEY CARDIGAN

by Claire Slade

FINISHED MEASUREMENTS
35 (39.5, 43.5, 47.75, 52.5, 57, 61.75)" finished bust circumference; meant to be worn with 4" positive ease
Sample is 39.5" size; model is 34" bust

YARN
Simply Wool™ (worsted weight, 100% Eco Wool; 219 yards/100g): Wallace 27472, 6 (8, 8, 9, 11, 11, 12) hanks

NEEDLES
US 7 (4.5mm) 32" or longer circular needles, or size to obtain gauge

NOTIONS
Yarn Needle
Cable Needle
20 Stitch Markers
Scrap Yarn or Stitch Holder

GAUGE
20 sts and 26 rows = 4" in Reverse Stockinette Stitch, blocked
24 sts and 26 rows = 4" over all Cable Patterns, blocked

For pattern support, contact verilyknits@gmail.com

Chalkney Cardigan

Notes:

Inspired by the woods from childhood memories, Chalkney is named after an ancient woodland, full of timeworn twisting trees and Roman trackways.

Designed to be worn without button closures, the fronts of this cardigan have extra width to allow for them to be wrapped over one another and secured with a pin if desired, or to just hang loose.

Chalkney is knit flat from the bottom up to the underarm, where sleeves and body are then joined and raglan decreases used to shape the upper section. The moss and cable border is then continued beyond the neck bind off to create a back collar.

Charts are worked flat; read RS rows (odd numbers) from right to left, and WS rows (even numbers) from left to right.

RM / PRM
Raglan Marker / Place Raglan Marker (use a unique color/type of marker from the others)

2/1 RC (2 over 1 right cable)
Sl1 to CN, hold in back; K2, K1 from CN.

2/1 LC (2 over 1 left cable)
Sl2 to CN, hold in front; K1, K2 from CN.

2/1 RPC (2 over 1 right cable, purl back)
Sl1 to CN, hold in back; K2, P1 from CN.

2/1 LPC (2 over 1 left cable, purl back)
Sl2 to CN, hold in front; P1, K2 from CN.

2/2 RC (2 over 2 right cable)
Sl2 to CN, hold in back; K2, K2 from CN.

2/2 LC (2 over 2 left cable)
Sl2 to CN, hold in front; K2, K2 from CN.

2/2 RPC (2 over 2 right cable, purl back)
Sl2 to CN, hold in back; K2, P2 from CN.

2/2 LPC (2 over 2 left cable, purl back)
Sl2 to CN, hold in front; P2, K2 from CN.

2/3 LC (2 over 3 left cable)
Sl2 to CN, hold in front; K3, K2 from CN.

2/3 RC (2 over 3 right cable)
Sl3 to CN, hold in back; K2, K3 from CN.

Moss Stitch (flat over an even number of sts)
Row 1 (RS): (K1, P1) to end.
Row 2 (WS): Rep Row 1.
Row 3: (P1, K1) to end.
Row 4: Rep Row 3.
Rep Rows 1-4 for pattern.

Right Edge Cable (flat over 19 sts)
Row 1 (RS): (P1, K1) three times, P1, 2/3 RC, (P1, K1) three times, P1.
Row 2 (WS): (K1, P1) three times, K1, P5, (K1, P1) three times, K1.
Row 3: (K1, P1) three times, 2/1 RC, P1, 2/1 LC, (P1, K1) three times.
Row 4: (P1, K1) three times, P3, K1, P3, (K1, P1) three times.
Row 5: (P1, K1) two times, P1, 2/1 RC, P1, K1, P1, 2/1 LC, (P1, K1) two times, P1.
Row 6: (K1, P1) two times, K1, P3, K1, P1, K1, P3, (K1, P1) two times, K1.
Row 7: (K1, P1) two times, 2/1 RC, (P1, K1) two times, P1, 2/1 LC, (P1, K1) two times.
Row 8: (P1, K1) two times, P3, (K1, P1) three times, P2, (K1, P1) two times.
Row 9: P1, K1, P1, 2/1 RC, (P1, K1) three times, P1, 2/1 LC, P1, K1, P1.
Row 10: K1, P1, K1, P3, (K1, P1) four times, P2, K1, P1, K1.
Row 11: K1, P1, 2/1 RC, (P1, K1) four times, P1, 2/1 LC, P1, K1.
Row 12: P1, K1, P3, (K1, P1) five times, P2, K1, P1.
Row 13: P1, K1, 2/1 LPC, (K1, P1) four times, K1, 2/1 RPC, K1, P1.
Row 14: K1, P1, K1, P3, (K1, P1) four times, P2, K1, P1, K1.
Row 15: K1, P1, K1, 2/1 LPC, (K1, P1) three times, K1, 2/1 RPC, K1, P1, K1.
Row 16: (P1, K1) two times, P3, (K1, P1) three times, P2, (K1, P1) two times.
Row 17: (P1, K1) two times, 2/1 LPC, (K1, P1) two times, K1, 2/1 RPC, (K1, P1) two times.
Row 18: (K1, P1) three times, P2, (K1, P1) two times, P2, (K1, P1) two times, K1.
Row 19: (K1, P1) two times, K1, 2/1 LPC, K1, P1, K1, 2/1 RPC, (K1, P1) two times, K1.
Row 20: (P1, K1) three times, P3, K1, P3, (K1, P1) three times.
Row 21: (P1, K1) three times, 2/1 LPC, K1, 2/1 RPC, (K1, P1) three times.
Row 22: (K1, P1) four times, P4, (K1, P1) three times, K1.
Row 23: (K1, P1) three times, K1, 2/3 RC, (K1, P1) three times, K1.
Row 24: (P1, K1) three times, P7, (K1, P1) three times.
Rep Rows 1-24 for pattern.

Left Edge Cable (flat over 19 sts)
Row 1 (RS): (K1, P1) three times, K1, 2/3 LC, (K1, P1) three times, K1.
Row 2 (WS): (P1, K1) three times, P7, (K1, P1) three times.
Row 3: (P1, K1) three times, 2/1 RPC, K1, 2/1 LPC, (K1, P1) three times.
Row 4: (K1, P1) three times, P2, K1, P1, K1, P3, (K1, P1) two times, K1.
Row 5: (K1, P1) two times, K1, 2/1 RPC, K1, P1, K1, 2/1 LPC, (K1, P1) two times, K1.
Row 6: (P1, K1) two times, P3, (K1, P1) three times, P2, (K1, P1) two times.
Row 7: (P1, K1) two times, 2/1 RPC, (K1, P1) two times, K1, 2/1 LPC, (K1, P1) two times.
Row 8: (K1, P1) two times, P2, (K1, P1) four times, P2, K1, P1, K1.

Row 9: K1, P1, K1, 2/1 RPC, (K1, P1) three times, K1, 2/1 LPC, K1, P1, K1.
Row 10: P1, K1, P3, (K1, P1) five times, P2, K1, P1.
Row 11: P1, K1, 2/1 RPC, (K1, P1) four times, K1, 2/1 LPC, K1, P1.
Row 12: K1, P3, (K1, P1) six times, P2, K1.
Row 13: K1, P1, 2/1 LC, (P1, K1) four times, P1, 2/1 RC, P1, K1.
Row 14: P1, K1, P3, (K1, P1) five times, P2, K1, P1.
Row 15: P1, K1, P1, 2/1 LC, (P1, K1) three times, P1, 2/1 RC, P1, K1, P1.
Row 16: (K1, P1) two times, P2, (K1, P1) four times, P2, K1, P1, K1.
Row 17: (K1, P1) two times, 2/1 LC, (P1, K1) two times, P1, 2/1 RC, (P1, K1) two times.
Row 18: (P1, K1) two times, P3, (K1, P1) three times, P2, (K1, P1) two times.
Row 19: (P1, K1) two times, P1, 2/1 LC, P1, K1, P1, 2/1 RC, (P1, K1) two times, P1.
Row 20: (K1, P1) three times, P2, K1, P1 K1, P3, (K1, P1) two times, K1.
Row 21: (K1, P1) three times, 2/1 LC, P1, 2/1 RC, (P1, K1) three times.
Row 22: (P1, K1) three times, P3, K1, P3, (K1, P1) three times.
Row 23: (P1, K1) three times, P1, 2/3 LC, (P1, K1) three times, P1.
Row 24: (K1, P1) four times, P4, (K1, P1) three times, K1.
Rep Rows 1-24 for pattern.

Braid Cable (flat over 12 sts)
Row 1 (RS): P3, K2, 2/2 LC, P3.
Row 2 (WS): K3, P6, K3.
Row 3: P3, 2/2 RC, K2, P3.
Row 4: Rep Row 2.
Row 5: P3, K2, 2/2 LC, P3.
Row 6: Rep Row 2.
Row 7: P3, 2/2 RPC, K2, P3.
Row 8: K3, P2, K2, P2, K3.
Row 9: P2, 2/1 RPC, P2, 2/1 LPC, P2.
Row 10: K2, P2, K4, P2, K2.
Row 11: P1, 2/1 RPC, P4, 2/1 LPC, P1.
Row 12: K1, P2, K6, P2, K1.
Row 13: P1, 2/1 LPC, P4, 2/1 RPC, P1.
Row 14: K2, P2, K4, P2, K2.
Row 15: P2, 2/1 LPC, P2, 2/1 RPC, P2.
Row 16: K3, P2, K2, P2, K3.
Row 17: P3, K2, 2/2 RC, P3.
Row 18: K3, P6, K3.
Row 19: P3, 2/2 RC, K2, P3.
Row 20: Rep Row 2.
Row 21: Rep Row 1.
Row 22: Rep Row 2.
Row 23: Rep Row 3.
Row 24: Rep Row 2.
Rep Rows 1-24 for pattern.

Back Panel Cable (flat over 52 sts)
Row 1 (RS): P1, 2/1 LPC, P9, 2/1 RPC, P2, 2/1 RPC, K1, 2/2 RPC, 2/2 LPC, K1, 2/1 LPC, P2, 2/1 LPC, P9, 2/1 RPC, P1.
Row 2 (WS): K2, P2, K9, P2, K3, P2, K1, P3, K4, P3, K1, P2, K3, P2, K9, P2, K2.
Row 3: P2, 2/1 LPC, P7, 2/1 RPC, P2, 2/1 RPC, K1, P1, K2, P4, K2, P1, K1, 2/1 LPC, P2, 2/1 LPC, P7, 2/1 RPC, P2.
Row 4: K3, P2, K7, P2, K3, P2, K1, P1, K1, P2, K4, P2, K1, P1, K1, P2, K3, P2, K7, P2, K3.
Row 5: P3, 2/1 LPC, P5, 2/1 RPC, P2, 2/1 RPC, K1, P1, K1, 2/2 LPC, 2/2 RPC, K1, P1, K1, 2/1 LPC, P2, 2/1 LPC, P5, 2/1 RPC, P3.
Row 6: K4, P2, K5, P2, K3, P2, (K1, P1) two times, K1, P6, (K1, P1) two times, K1, P2, K3, P2, K5, P2, K4.
Row 7: P4, 2/1 LPC, P3, 2/1 RPC, P2, 2/1 RPC, (K1, P1) three times, 2/2 RC, (P1, K1) three times, 2/1 LPC, P2, 2/1 LPC, P3, 2/1 RPC, P4.
Row 8: K5, P2, K3, P1, K4, P2, (K1, P1) three times, K1, P4, (K1, P1) three times, K1, (P2, K3) two times, P2, K5.
Row 9: P5, 2/1 LPC, P1, 2/1 RPC, P2, 2/1 RPC, (K1, P1) two times, K1, 2/2 RPC, 2/2 LPC, (K1, P1) two times, K1, 2/1 LPC, P2, 2/1 LPC, P1, 2/1 RPC, P5.
Row 10: K6, P2, K1, P2, K3, P2, (K1, P1) two times, K1, P3, K4, P3, (K1, P1) two times, K1, P2, K3, P2, K1, P2, K6.
Row 11: P6, 2/3 RC, P2, 2/1 RPC, (K1, P1) 3, times K2, P4, K2, (P1, K1) three times, 2/1 LPC, P2, 2/3 LC, P6.
Row 12: K6, P5, K2, P2, (K1, P1) three times, K1, P2, K4, P2, (K1, P1) three times, K1, P2, K2, P5, K6.
Row 13: P6, 2/3 RC, P2, 2/1 LPC, (P1, K1) three times, 2/2 LPC, 2/2 RPC, (K1, P1) three times, 2/1 RPC, P2, 2/3 LC, P6.
Row 14: K6, P5, K3, P2, (K1, P1) three times, K1, P6, (K1, P1) three times, K1, P2, K3, P5, K6.
Row 15: P5, 2/1 RPC, P1, 2/1 LPC, P2, 2/1 LPC, (P1, K1) three times, P1, 2/2 RC, (P1, K1) three times, P1, 2/1 RPC, P2, 2/1 RPC, P1, 2/1 LPC, P5.
Row 16: K5, (P2, K3) two times, P2, (K1, P1) three times, K1, P4, (K1, P1) three times, K1, (P2, K3) two times, P2, K5.
Row 17: P4, 2/1 RPC, P3, 2/1 LPC, P2, 2/1 LPC, (P1, K1) two times, 2/2 RPC, 2/2 LPC, (K1, P1) two times, 2/1 RPC, P2, 2/1 RPC, P3, 2/1 LPC, P4.
Row 18: K4, P2, K5, P2, K3, P2, K1, P1, K1, P3, K4, P3, K1, P1, K1, P2, K3, P2, K5, P2, K4.
Row 19: P3, 2/1 RPC, P5, 2/1 LPC, P2, 2/1 LPC, P1, K1, P1, K2, P4, K2, P1, K1, P1, 2/1 RPC, P2, 2/1 RPC, P5, 2/1 LPC, P3.
Row 20: K3, P2, K7, P2, K3, P2, K1, P1, K1, P2, K4, P2, K1, P1, K1, P2, K3, P2, K7, P2, K3.
Row 21: P2, 2/1 RPC, P7, 2/1 LPC, P2, 2/1 LPC, P1, K1, 2/2 LPC, 2/2 RPC, K1, P1, 2/1 RPC, P2, 2/1 RPC, P7, 2/1 LPC, P2.
Row 22: K2, P2, K9, P2, K3, P2, K1, P1, K1, P6, K1, P1, K1, P2, K3, P2, K9, P2, K2.
Row 23: P1, 2/1 RPC, P9, 2/1 LPC, P2, 2/1 LPC, P1, K1, P1, 2/2 RC, P1, K1, P1, 2/1 RPC, P2, 2/1 RPC, P9, 2/1 LPC, P1.
Row 24: K1, P2, K11, P2, K3, P2, K1, P1, K1, P4, K1, P1, K1, P2, K3, P2, K11, P2, K1.
Rep Rows 1-24 for pattern.

DIRECTIONS

Lower Edge
CO 222 (244, 264, 286, 310, 332, 356) sts.
Row 1 (RS): Work Row 1 of Right Edge Cable, PM, work Moss Stitch to last 19 sts, PM, work Row 1 of Left Edge Cable.
Row 2 (WS): Work next row of Left Edge Cable, SM, work Moss Stitch to M, SM, work next row of Right Edge Cable.
Row 3: Work next row of Right Edge Cable, SM, work Moss Stitch to M, SM, work next row of Left Edge Chart.
Rep Rows 2-3 until Rows 1-23 of Edge Cables have been worked.

Row 24 (WS): Work Row 24 of Left Edge Cable, SM, K12 (15, 17, 20, 23, 26, 29), PM, K12, PM, K18 (21, 23, 26, 29, 32, 35), PM for side, K9 (14, 20, 25, 31, 36, 42), PM, K12, PM, K3, PM, K52, PM, K3, PM, K12, PM, K9 (14, 20, 25, 31, 36, 42), PM for side, K18 (21, 23, 26, 29, 32, 35), PM, K12, PM, K12 (15, 17, 20, 23, 26, 29), SM, work Row 24 of Right Edge Cable.

Body
Row 1 (RS): Work Right Edge Cable, SM, P to M, SM, work Braid Cable, SM, P to M, SM, P to M, SM, work Braid Cable, SM, P to M, SM, work Back Panel Cable, SM, P to M, SM, work Braid Cable, SM, P to M, SM, P to M, SM, work Braid Cable, SM, P to M, SM, work Left Edge Cable.
Row 2 (WS): Work Left Edge Cable, SM, K to M, SM, work Braid Cable, SM, K to M, SM, K to M, SM, work Braid Cable, SM, K to M, SM, work Back Panel Cable, SM, K to M, SM, work Braid Cable, SM, K to M, SM, K to M, SM, work Braid Cable, SM, K to M, SM, work Left Edge Cable.

Rep Rows 1-2 until work measures 22" ending on a WS row; AT THE SAME TIME work body shaping decs on every fifth RS row as follows.
Dec Row (RS): (Work in pattern as set to 3 sts before side M, P2tog, P1, SM, P1, P2tog) two times, work in pattern as set to end. 4 sts dec.
Work Dec Row a total of six times. 198 (220, 240, 262, 286, 308, 332) sts.

Next Row: *Work in pattern to 2 (3, 3, 4, 4, 5, 6) sts before side M, BO next 4 (6, 6, 8, 8, 10, 12) sts; rep from * once more, work in pattern to end. 190 (208, 228, 246, 270, 288, 308). Place all remaining sts on scrap yarn.

Sleeves (make two the same)
CO 54 (60, 64, 66, 68, 72, 74) sts.
Work in Moss Stitch for 2" ending on a RS row.
Next Row (WS): K21 (24, 26, 27, 28, 30, 31), PM, K12, PM, K to end.
Next Row (RS): P to M, SM, work Braid Cable, SM, P to end.
Next Row: K to M, SM, work Braid Cable, SM, K to end.

Sleeve Increase Section
Row 1 (RS): P1, PFB, P to M, SM, work Braid Cable, SM, P to last 2 sts, PFB, P1. 2 sts inc.
WE as established for 15 (13, 11, 7, 7, 7, 5) rows.
Rep these 16 (14, 12, 8, 8, 8, 6) rows 5 (6, 7, 10, 11, 12, 14) more times. 66 (74, 80, 88, 92, 98, 104) sts.

WE as established until sleeve measures 20" or desired length to underarm, ending on a RS row.
Next 2 Rows: BO 2 (3, 3, 4, 4, 5, 6) sts, work as set to end. 62 (68, 74, 80, 84, 88, 92) sts.

Raglan
Setup Row (WS): Work in pattern as set across 53 (58, 62, 67, 73, 78, 83) left front sts, PRM, work in pattern as set across 62 (68, 74, 80, 84, 88, 92) sleeve sts, PRM, work in pattern as set across 84 (92, 104, 112, 124, 132, 142) back sts, PRM, work in pattern as set across 62 (68, 74, 80, 84, 88, 92) sleeve sts, PRM, work in pattern as set across 53 (58, 62, 67, 73, 78, 83) right front sts. 314 (344, 376, 406, 438, 464, 492) sts.
Row 1 (RS): (Work in pattern as set to 3 sts before RM, P2tog, P1, SM, P2tog, work in pattern as set to 2 sts before RM, P2tog, SM, P1, P2tog) two times, work in pattern as set to end. 4 sts dec.
Row 2 (WS): Work in pattern as set to end.
Rep Rows 1-2 15 (16, 18, 17, 15, 12, 11) more times. 186 (208, 224, 262, 310, 360, 396) sts.

Raglan & Neck Decrease Section
Row 1 (RS): Work in pattern across first 19 sts, SM, P2tog, (work in pattern as set to 3 sts before RM, P2tog, P1, SM, P2tog, work in pattern as set to 2 sts before RM, P2tog, SM, P1, P2tog) two times, work in pattern to 2 sts before final M, P2tog, SM, work in pattern to end. 10 sts dec.
Row 2 (WS): WE in pattern to end.
Rep Rows 1-2 6 (8, 9, 12, 16, 20, 23) more times. 116 (118, 124, 132, 140, 150, 156) sts.

Next Row (RS): (Work in pattern as set to 3 sts before RM, P2tog, P1, SM, P2tog, work in pattern as set to 2 sts before RM, P2tog, SM, P1, P2tog) two times, work in pattern as set to end. 108 (110, 116, 124, 132, 142, 148) sts.
Next Row (WS): WE in pattern to end.
Next Row (RS): Work in pattern across first 19 sts and place on scrap yarn, BO next 70, 72, 78, 86, 94, 104, 110) sts, work in pattern across final 19 sts.

Collar
Cont to work in pattern across 19 sts of Left Edge until work measures approx 6.25 (6.5, 7, 8, 8.5, 9.5, 10)" from neck BO edge, ending on a WS row; place all sts on scrap yarn.
Return held 19 sts of Right Edge to needle and work as for Left Edge.
Return Left Edge sts to needle and join both ends tog using Kitchener Stitch.

Finishing
Sew up both sleeve seams and underarm seams.
Sew the collar to the neck BO edge.
Weave in all ends, wash, and block to diagram.

A 39.75 (44.25, 48.25, 52.5, 57.5, 61.75, 66.5)"
B 35 (39.5, 43.5, 47.75, 52.5, 57, 61.75)"
C 10.5 (11.5, 12.5, 12.75, 13.25, 14, 14.5)"
D 13 (14.5, 15.5, 17.25, 18, 19.25, 20.5)"
E 7.5 (8.25, 9.25, 10, 10.5, 10.75, 11.5)" (raglan depth)
F 20"
G 22"

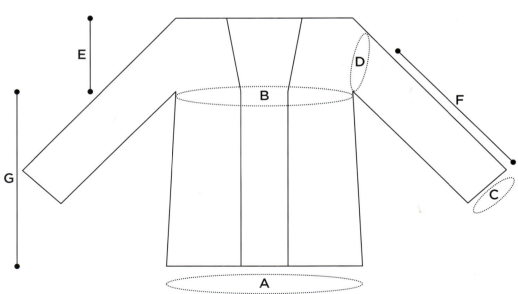

LEGEND

☐ **K**
RS: Knit stitch
WS: Purl stitch

⊡ **P**
RS: Purl stitch
WS: Knit stitch

Cable 2 Over 1 Right (2/1 RC)
Sl1 to CN, hold in back; K2, K1 from CN

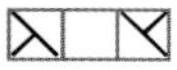

Cable 2 Over 1 Left (2/1 LC)
Sl2 to CN, hold in front; K1, K2 from CN

Cable 2 Over 1 Right, Purl back (2/1 RPC)
Sl1 to CN, hold in back; K2, P1 from CN

Cable 2 Over 1 Left, Purl back (2/1 LPC)
Sl2 to CN, hold in front; P1, K2 from CN

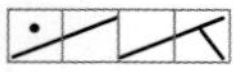

Cable 2 Over 2 Right, Purl back (2/2 RPC)
Sl2 to CN, hold in back; K2, P2 from CN

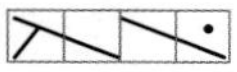

Cable 2 Over 2 Left, Purl back (2/2 LPC)
Sl2 to CN, hold in front; P2, K2 from CN

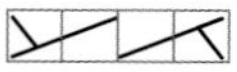

Cable 2 Over 2 Right (2/2 RC)
Sl2 to CN, hold in back; K2, K2 from CN

Cable 2 Over 2 Left (2/2 LC)
Sl2 to CN, hold in front; K2, K2 from CN

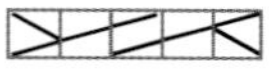

Cable 2 Over 3 Right (2/3 RC)
Sl3 to CN, hold in back; K2, K3 from CN

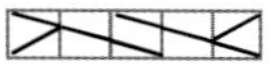

Cable 2 Over 3 Left (2/3 LC)
Sl3 to CN, hold in front; K3, K2 from CN

Right Edge Cable

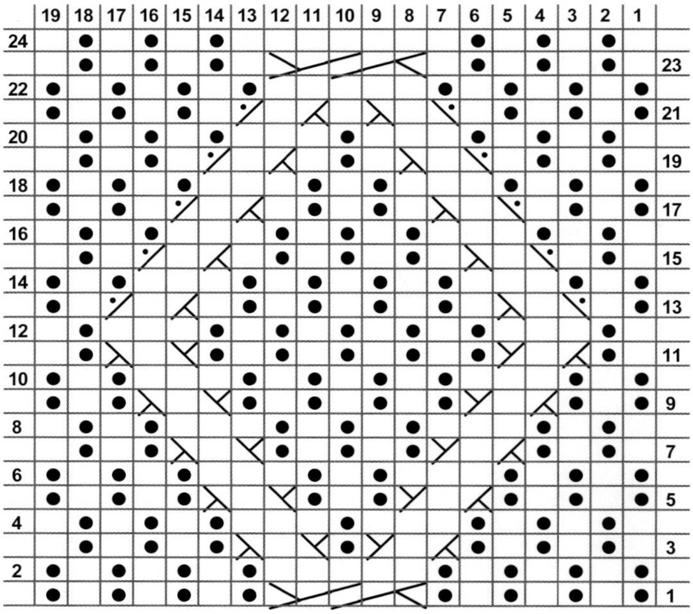

Left Edge Cable

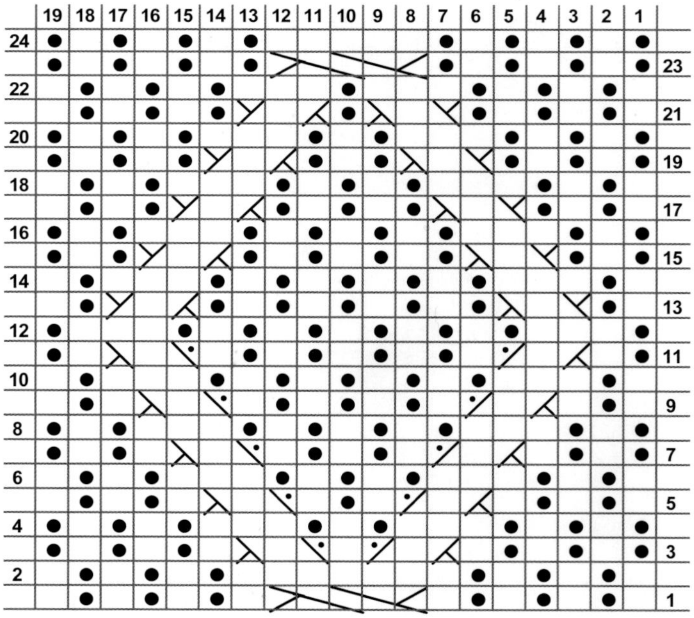

Braid Cable

Charles Dixon
8523 199th Pl SW
Edmonds, WA 98026

Back Panel

CLUTHAR HAT

by Joan E. Beck

FINISHED MEASUREMENTS
Approximately 21.75" (Grafted version) or 22" (Three Needle BO version) circumference × 8" height; to fit adult 21"-23" head circumference

YARN
Twill™ (worsted weight, 100% Superwash Merino Wool; 149 yards/100g): Gold Rush 27934, 2 hanks

NEEDLES
US 6 (4mm) 16" circular needles, and DPNs or two 24" circular needles for two circulars technique or 32" or longer circular needles for Magic Loop technique, or size to obtain gauge
US 4 (3.5mm) 16" circular needles or two 24" circular needles for two circulars technique or 32" or longer circular needles for Magic Loop technique, or two sizes smaller than size used to obtain gauge

NOTIONS
Yarn Needle
Removable Stitch Markers
Scrap Yarn for Provisional Cast On
Comparable Size Crochet Hook for Provisional Cast On

GAUGE
16 sts (1 repeat) = 2.5" and 41 rows = 4" in Slip Cross Open Cable Band on larger needles, blocked (row gauge for Slip Cross Open Cable Band is extremely important to achieve correct size: two repeats of chart = 2.75")
21 sts and 44 rnds = 4" of Mock Honeycomb Chart on larger needles, blocked (Mock Honeycomb gauge can vary slightly depending upon length of 3-stitch floats: the shorter the floats, the more textured the stitch pattern)

For pattern support, contact TooeyB6@gmail.com

Cluthar Hat

Notes:
The combination of textured patterns gives this hat its Cluthar—"comfortable as in warmth"—with a thick, cozy band and a deeply-textured body to keep it snuggly and warm.

The hat starts with a sideways-knitted brim, which is joined with a choice of either invisibly grafting live stitches to cast on edge or with a 3-Needle Bind Off. Stitches are picked up along the edge and a ribbed facing is knit for added warmth. Next, the honeycomb-textured body flows seamlessly from the ribbing and the crown is shaped with slip-stitch decreases.

Slip Cross Open Cable Band chart is worked flat; read RS rows (even numbers) from right to left, and WS rows (odd numbers) from left to right—chart begins with a WS row. Mock Honeycomb and Crown Shaping charts are worked in the round; read each chart row from right to left as a RS row.

TwK (twisted knit stitch)
Sl st K-wise, return to LH needle, K1.

1/2 RDSC (1/2 right drop stitch cable)
Slip next two sts P-wise, drop next st off needle to front, return the two slipped sts to LH needle, return dropped st to LH needle, K3.

1/2 LDSC (1/2 left drop stitch cable)
Drop st to front, K2, return dropped st to LH needle, K1.

2/2 CDSC (2/2 center drop stitch cable)
Drop st off LH needle, slip 2 sts P-wise to RH needle, drop next st, return first dropped st to LH needle, slip the two slipped sts back to LH needle, return second dropped st to LH needle, K4.

KU2 (knit under 2 strands)
Insert RH needle under two previous floats, K1, bring RH needle back under floats.

MMR (move marker right)
Preparation for CDD: Work to one st before M, Sl st to RH needle, remove M, Sl st back to LH needle, replace M.

Slip Cross Open Cable Band (flat over 16 sts)
Row 1 (WS): Sl2 WYIF, K2, P1, K6, P1, K2, Sl1 WYIF, K1.
Row 2 (RS): K1, TwK, K2, Sl1 WYIB, K6, Sl1 WYIB, K2, K2 TBL.
Row 3: Sl2 WYIF, K2, Sl1 WYIF, K6, Sl1 WYIF, K2, Sl1 WYIF, K1.
Row 4: K1, TwK, K2, 1/2 LDSC, K2, 1/2 RDSC, K2, K2 TBL.
Row 5: Sl2 WYIF, K4, P1, K2, P1, K4, Sl1 WYIF, K1.
Row 6: K1, TwK, K4, Sl1 WYIB, K2, Sl1 WYIB, K4, K2 TBL.
Row 7: Sl2 WYIF, K4, Sl1 WYIF, K2, Sl1 WYIF, K4, Sl1 WYIF, K1.
Row 8: K1, TwK, K4, 2/2 CDSC, K4, K2 TBL.
Row 9: Rep Row 5.
Row 10: Rep Row 6.
Row 11: Rep Row 7.
Row 12: K1, TwK, K2, 1/2 RDSC, K2, 1/2 LDSC, K2, K2 TBL.
Row 13: Rep Row 1.
Row 14: K1, TwK, K12, K2 TBL.
Rep Rows 1-14 for pattern.

Grafting Live Stitches to a Cast On Edge
Live sts on front needle are worked as for front needle instructions for normal Kitchener Stitch. Back is worked in pattern: work yarn under base of knit sts (yarn travels over Long Tail Cast On); for purl sts, insert yarn needle under front strand of Long Tail Cast On, over base of purl st, then back under next front Long Tail Cast On strand. Each strand is worked into two times.
Setup: Pass yarn needle through first st on front needle as to P, leave on needle.
Pair 1: Back Needle (BN)—Insert yarn needle right to left under base of K st; Front Needle (FN)—K off needle, P leaving on needle (same as normal Kitchener).
Pair 2: BN—Insert needle left to right under base of K st (twisted st); FN—K off, P on.
Pair 3: BN—Insert needle under front strand of Long Tail Cast On (LTCO), over base of purl st, then back under next front LTCO strand; FN—K off, P on.
Pair 4: Rep Pair 3.
Pair 5: Rep Pair 1.
Pairs 6-11: Rep Pair 3.
Pair 12: Rep Pair 1.
Pairs 13-14: Rep Pair 3.
Pair 15: Rep Pair 1.
Pair 16: Rep Pair 1.
Knit off the final front live st.

Mock Honeycomb (in the round over 112 sts, a multiple of 4)
Rnd 1: K all. 112 sts.
Rnd 2: (K1, Sl3 WYIF) 28 times.
Rnd 3: K all.
Rnds 4-5: Rep Rnds 2-3.
Rnd 6: (K2, KU2, K1) 28 times.
Rnd 7: K to 1 st before BOR M, Sl1 WYIF.
Rnd 8: Sl2 WYIF, (K1, Sl3 WYIF) 27 times, K2.
Rnds 9-10: Rep Rnds 7-8.
Rnd 11: K all.
Rnd 12: (KU2, K3) 28 times.
Rep Rnds 1-12 for pattern.

DIRECTIONS

Brim
Choose between two methods for joining the brim band: grafting live sts to the cast on row for an invisible join, or the 3-Needle Bind Off method. (Note: grafting with a Provisional Cast On is not a recommended method because, due to the garter stitch and cable combination, it would not be invisible.)

Grafted Version
With larger needles, CO 16 sts using a Long Tail Cast On. Work Slip Cross Open Cable Band chart 16 times, ending last rep on Row 11 (WS). Band measures approx 21.75".

In preparation for grafting, rearrange sts on needle as follows (do not work) (RS): Sl1, Sl1 K-wise, Sl4, drop next st off needle, Sl2 from RH needle back to LH needle, place dropped st onto RH needle, Sl4, drop next st off needle, Sl2, place dropped st onto RH needle, Sl2, Sl2 back to front as if to P TBL.

Break yarn, leaving an approx 20" tail for working the graft. Arrange work so that CO edge is above/behind the live sts, working yarn at front right. Work Grafting Live Stitches to a Cast On Edge instructions. Proceed to Body instructions.

3-Needle Bind Off Version

With larger needles, CO 16 sts with a Provisional Cast On (crochet method).

Setup Row (RS): K across.

Work Slip Cross Open Cable Band chart 16 times, ending last rep on Row 13 (WS). Band measures approx 22". Unravel the scrap yarn and put resulting 15 sts on needle. PU 1 st in the Garter St edge. 16 sts. With RSs tog, work 3-Needle Bind Off. Break yarn. Proceed to Body instructions.

Body

Turn band inside-out (WS facing) and position Garter Stitch edge on top. Counting to the left from join, PM for new BOR between 11th and 12th purl bump.

Change to smaller needles. Joining yarn at new BOR, PU and K 110 sts through each purl bump of Garter Stitch edge plus 2 more sts at join. 112 sts.

Work 2x2 Rib in the rnd for approx 16 rnds, or 2.25" from band.

Change to larger needles. Work Mock Honeycomb from chart or written rows three times (36 rnds), ending 1 st before BOR M on last rep. Piece measures approx 3.25" from end of 2x2 Rib.

Crown Shaping

Mark shaping points as follows: from BOR M, (count 28 sts to the left, PM) three times. There will be four 28-st sections. Work Crown Shaping from chart or written rows below, moving each M one st to the right before working each CDD (odd rnds) as noted in rows, and switching to DPNs when needed.

Rnd 1: (MMR, CDD, K25) four times. SM. 104 sts.
Rnd 2: *Sl1, K2, (K1, Sl3 WYIF) five times, K3, SM; rep from * three more times, end last rep K2.
Rnd 3: (MMR, CDD, K23) four times. SM. 96 sts.
Rnd 4: *Sl1, K1, (K1, Sl3 WYIF) five times, K2, SM; rep from * three more times, end last rep K1.
Rnd 5: (MMR, CDD, K21) four times. SM. 88 sts.
Rnd 6: *Sl1, K2, (KU2, K3) four times, KU2, K2, SM; rep from * three more times, end last rep K1.
Rnd 7: (MMR, CDD, K19) four times. SM. 80 sts.
Rnd 8: *Sl1, K1, (K1, Sl3 WYIF) four times, K2, SM; rep from * three more times, end last rep K1.
Rnd 9: (MMR, CDD, K17) four times. SM. 72 sts.
Rnd 10: *Sl1, (K1, Sl3 WYIF) four times, K1, SM; rep from * three more times, end last rep K0.
Rnd 11: (MMR, CDD, K15) four times. SM. 64 sts.
Rnd 12: *Sl1, K1, (KU2, K3) three times, KU2, K1, SM; rep from * three more times, end last rep K0.
Rnd 13: (MMR, CDD, K13) four times. SM. 56 sts.
Rnd 14: (Sl1, K1, P2, K2, Sl3 WYIF, K2, P2, K1, SM) four times, end last rep K0.
Rnd 15: (MMR, CDD, K11) four times. SM. 48 sts.
Rnd 16: (Sl1, K1, P2, K1, Sl3 WYIF, K1, P2, K1, SM) four times, end last rep K0.
Rnd 17: (MMR, CDD, K9) four times. SM. 40 sts.
Rnd 18: (Sl1, K1, P2, K1, KU2, K1, P2, K1, SM) four times, end last rep K0.
Rnd 19: (MMR, CDD, K7) four times. SM. 32 sts.
Rnd 20: *Sl1, (K1, P2) two times, K1, SM; rep from * three more times, end last rep K0.
Rnd 21: (MMR, CDD, K5) four times. SM. 24 sts.
Rnd 22: (Sl1, K1, P3, K1, SM) four times, end last rep K0.
Rnd 23: (MMR, CDD, K3) four times. SM. 16 sts.
Rnd 24: (Sl1, K1, P1, K1, SM) four times, end last rep K0.
Rnd 25: (MMR, CDD, K1) four times. 8 sts.

Break yarn, thread through remaining 8 sts and fasten off.

Finishing

Weave in ends and wash. To preserve the texture of the Mock Honeycomb and the 2x2 Rib, do not stretch while drying.

LEGEND

■ **No Stitch**
Placeholder—no stitch made

□ **K**
RS: Knit stitch
WS: Purl stitch

• **P**
RS: Purl stitch
WS: Knit stitch

V **Sl**
RS: Slip stitch purl-wise, with yarn in back
WS: Slip stitch purl-wise, with yarn in front

V̱ **Sl WYIF**
Slip stitch purl-wise, with yarn in front

B **K TBL**
Knit stitch through the back loop

1 over 2 Left Drop Stitch Cable (1/2 LDSC)
Drop st to front, K2, return dropped st to left-hand needle and knit it

1 over 2 Right Drop Stitch Cable (1/2 RDSC)
Sl2, drop next st off needle to front, return 2 slipped sts to left-hand needle, return dropped st to left-hand needle, knit the 3 sts

2 over 2 Center Drop Stitch Cable (1/2 CDSC)
Drop st to front, Sl2 to right-hand needle, drop st to front, return first dropped st to left-hand needle, return 2 slipped sts to left-hand needle, return second dropped st to left-hand needle, knit the 4 sts

Twisted Knit Stitch (TwK)
Slip stitch knit-wise, return to left-hand needle, knit the stitch

CDD
Slip first and second stitches together as if to K2tog; knit 1 stitch; pass 2 slipped stitches over the knit stitch

SM
Slip stitch marker

MMR
Move stitch marker 1 stitch to the right

KU2
Knit under 2 strands (see *Notes*)

Stitch for next rnd
On the last repeat, this stitch will be used in the CDD on the next round

Pattern Repeat

Slip Cross Open Cable Band

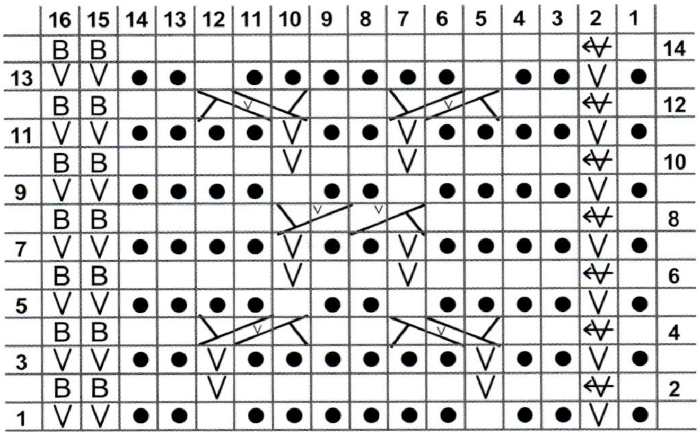

16	15	14	13	12	11	10	9	8	7	6	5	4	3	2	1	
B	B													⋈		14
		V	V	•	•	•	•	•	•	•	•	•	•	V	•	13
B	B				╳╳			╳╳						⋈		12
		V	V	•	•	•	•	•	•	•	•	•	•	V	•	11
B	B					V			V					⋈		10
		V	V	•	•	•	•	•	•	•	•	•	•	V	•	9
B	B					╳╳╳╳								⋈		8
		V	V	•	•	•	V	•	V	•	•	•	•	V	•	7
B	B					V			V					⋈		6
		V	V	•	•	•	•	•	•	•	•	•	•	V	•	5
B	B				╳╳			╳╳						⋈		4
		V	V	•	•	•	•	•	•	•	•	•	•	V	•	3
B	B					V			V					⋈		2
		V	V	•	•	•	•	•	•	•	•	•	•	V	•	1

Mock Honeycomb

8	7	6	5	4	3	2	1	
			⋇				⋇	12
								11
		V	V		V	V		10
V								9
		V	V		V	V		8
V								7
	⋇			⋇				6
								5
V	V	V		V	V	V		4
								3
V	V	V		V	V	V		2
								1

Cluthar Hat

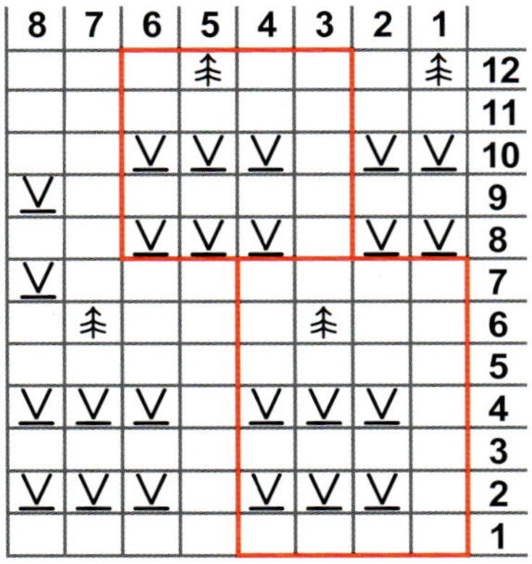

Crown Shaping

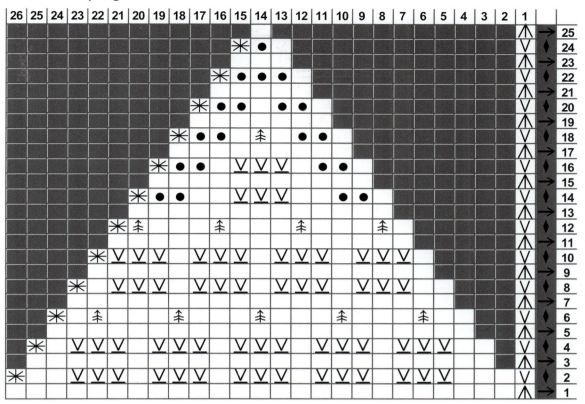

COPPICE MITTS

by Claire Slade

FINISHED MEASUREMENTS
8.5" length × 7.5" circumference

YARN
Palette™ (fingering weight, 100% Peruvian Highland Wool; 231 yards/50g): Turmeric 24251, 1 ball

NEEDLES
US 2.5 (3mm) DPNs, or size to obtain gauge

NOTIONS
Yarn Needle
3 Stitch Markers
Cable Needle
Scrap Yarn or Stitch Holder

GAUGE
44 sts and 46 rnds = 4" in Twist Cable Pattern in the round, blocked
30 sts and 46 rnds = 4" in Twisted Rib Pattern in the round, blocked

For pattern support, contact verilyknits@gmail.com

Coppice Mitts

Notes:
Coppicing is an ancient method of forest management involving cutting trees back so that they form new growth. Inspired by this tradition, these mitts are formed with tiny cables that grow and intertwine to form an intricate twisting pattern.

The left and right mitt each has its own chart. Charts are worked in the round from the bottom up; read all chart rows from right to left as RS rows.

M1P (make 1 purl stitch)
Inserting LH needle from back to front, PU horizontal strand between st just worked and next st, and P into it.

RT-TBL2 (right twist, both stitches through back loop)
Sl1 to CN, hold in back, K1 TBL, K1 TBL from CN.

RPT-TBL (right twist, purl back, front through back loop)
Sl1 to CN, hold in back, K1 TBL, P1 from CN.

LPT-TBL (left twist, purl back, front through back loop)
Sl1 to CN, hold in front, P1, K1 TBL from CN.

DIRECTIONS

Left Mitt
CO 68 sts and join to work in the rnd, being careful not to twist sts; PM for BOR.

Cuff
Rnd 1: P1, K1 TBL, P1, K2 TBL, (P1, K1 TBL) seven times, P2, (K1 TBL, P1, K1 TBL, P2) two times, K1 TBL, (P1, K1 TBL) to end.
Rnd 2: P1, K1 TBL, P1, RT-TBL2, (P1, K1 TBL) seven times, P2, (K1 TBL, P1, K1 TBL, P2) two times, K1 TBL, (P1, K1 TBL) to end.
Rep Rnds 1-2 until work measures 2.5" ending on a Rnd 1.

Next Rnd: P1, K1 TBL, P1, RT-TBL2, (P1, K1 TBL) seven times, P2, (K1 TBL, P1, K1 TBL, P2) two times, (K1 TBL, P1) six times, PM, K1 TBL, (P1, K1 TBL) to end.

Thumb Increases
Rnd 1: Work Left Mitt Chart to M, SM, K1 TBL, (P1, K1 TBL) to end.
Rep Rnd 1 until all 34 rnds of Left Mitt Chart have been worked. 84 sts.

Hand
Rnd 1: P1, K1 TBL, place next 20 sts on scrap yarn for thumb, CO 4 sts, K1 TBL, PM, work Rnd 1 of Hand Chart to M, SM, K1 TBL, (P1, K1 TBL) to end. 68 sts.
Rnd 2: P1, K1 TBL, P4, K1 TBL, SM, work Rnd 2 of Hand Chart to M, SM, K1 TBL, (P1, K1 TBL) to end.
Rnd 3: P1, LPT-TBL, P2, RPT-TBL, SM, work Rnd 3 of Hand Chart to M, SM, K1 TBL, (P1, K1 TBL) to end.
Rnd 4: P2, LPT-TBL, RPT-TBL, P1, SM, work Rnd 4 of Hand Chart to M, SM, K1 TBL, (P1, K1 TBL) to end.
Rnd 5: P3, K2 TBL, P2, SM, work next rnd of Hand Chart to M, SM, K1 TBL, (P1, K1 TBL) to end.
Rnd 6: P3, RT-TBL2, P2, SM, work next rnd of Hand Chart to M, SM, K1 TBL, (P1, K1 TBL) to end.
Rep Rnds 5-6 until all 26 rnds of Hand Chart have been worked.

Upper Edge
Rnd 1: P1, K1 TBL, P1, K2 TBL, (P1, K1 TBL) seven times, P2, (K1 TBL, P1, K1 TBL, P2) two times, K1 TBL, (P1, K1 TBL) to end.
Rnd 2: P1, K1 TBL, P1, RT-TBL2, (P1, K1 TBL) seven times, P2, (K1 TBL, P1, K1 TBL, P2) two times, K1 TBL, (P1, K1 TBL) to end.
Rep Rnds 1-2 once, then Rnd 1 once more.
BO all sts in pattern.

Right Mitt
CO 68 sts and join to work in the rnd, being careful not to twist sts; PM for BOR.

Cuff
Rnd 1: (P1, K1 TBL) six times, (P2, K1 TBL, P1, K1 TBL) two times, P2, (K1 TBL, P1) seven times, K2 TBL, (P1, K1 TBL) to end.
Rnd 2: (P1, K1 TBL) six times, (P2, K1 TBL, P1, K1 TBL) two times, P2, (K1 TBL, P1) seven times, RT-TBL2, (P1, K1 TBL) to end.
Rep Rnds 1-2 until work measures 2.5" ending on a Rnd 1.

Next Rnd: (P1, K1 TBL) six times, (P2, K1 TBL, P1, K1 TBL) two times, P2, (K1 TBL, P1) seven times, RT-TBL2, P1, K1 TBL, P1, PM, K1 TBL, (P1, K1 TBL) to end.

Thumb Increases
Rnd 1: Work Right Mitt Chart to M, SM, K1 TBL, (P1, K1 TBL) to end.
Rep Rnd 1 until all 34 rnds of Right Mitt Chart have been worked. 84 sts.

Hand
Rnd 1: Work Rnd 1 of Hand Chart across first 36 sts, PM, K1 TBL, place next 20 sts on scrap yarn for thumb, CO 4 sts, K1 TBL, P1, PM, K1 TBL, (P1, K1 TBL) to end. 68 sts.
Rnd 2: Work Rnd 2 of Hand Chart, SM, K1 TBL, P4, K1 TBL, P1, SM, K1 TBL, (P1, K1 TBL) to end.
Rnd 3: Work Rnd 3 of Hand Chart, SM, LPT-TBL, P2, RPT-TBL, P1, SM, K1 TBL, (P1, K1 TBL) to end.
Rnd 4: Work Rnd 4 of Hand Chart, SM, P1, LPT-TBL, RPT-TBL, P2, SM, K1 TBL, (P1, K1 TBL) to end.
Rnd 5: Work next rnd of Hand Chart, SM, P2, K2 TBL, P3, SM, K1 TBL, (P1, K1 TBL) to end.
Rnd 6: Work next rnd of Hand Chart, SM, P2, RT-TBL2, P3, SM, K1 TBL, (P1, K1 TBL) to end.
Rep Rnds 5-6 until all 26 rnds of Hand Chart have been worked.

Upper Edge
Rnd 1: (P1, K1 TBL) six times, (P2, K1 TBL, P1, K1 TBL) two times, P2, (K1 TBL, P1) seven times, K2 TBL, (P1, K1 TBL) to end.
Rnd 2: (P1, K1 TBL) six times, (P2, K1 TBL, P1, K1 TBL) two times, P2, (K1 TBL, P1) seven times, RT-TBL2, (P1, K1 TBL) to end.
Rep Rnds 1-2 once, then Rnd 1 once more.
BO all sts in pattern.

Thumb (both worked the same)
With RS facing, return the held 20 sts to needles and rejoin yarn.
PU and K 3 sts across gap, PM for BOR. 23 sts.
Rnd 1: P1, (K1 TBL, P1) four times, K2 TBL, (P1, K1 TBL) to end.
Rnd 2: P1, (K1 TBL, P1) four times, RT-TBL2, (P1, K1 TBL) to end.
Rep Rnds 1-2 six more times.
BO all sts in pattern.

Finishing
Weave in ends, wash, and block to measurements.

LEGEND

▪ **No Stitch**
Placeholder—no stitch made

• **Purl Stitch**

B **K TBL**
Knit stitch through the back loop

MR **M1R**
Make 1 right-leaning stitch

M **M1L**
Make 1 left-leaning stitch

MP **M1P**
Make 1 purl stitch

Right Twist, TBL, Purl back (RPT-TBL)
Sl1 to CN, hold in back; K1 through back loop, P1 from CN

Left Twist, TBL, Purl back (LPT-TBL)
Sl1 to CN, hold in front; P1, K1 through back loop from CN

Right Twist, TBL both sts (RT-TBL2)
Sl1 to CN, hold in back; K1 through back loop, K1 through back loop from CN

Left Twist, TBL both sts (LT-TBL2)
Sl1 to CN, hold in front; K1 through back loop, K1 through back loop from CN

Hand Chart

Left Mitt Chart

Right Mitt Chart

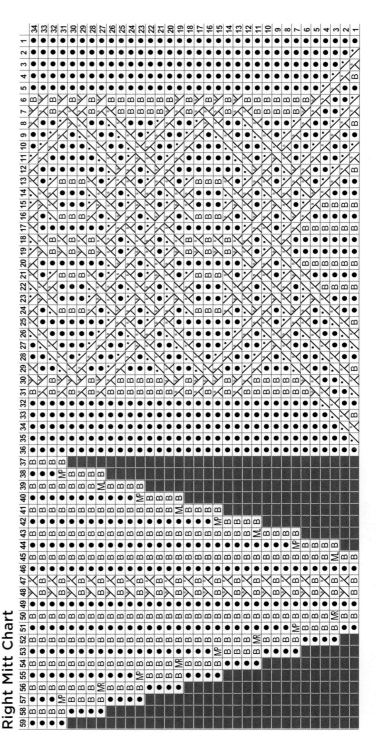

Coppice Mitts 37

KELLS WRAP

by Allison Griffith

FINISHED MEASUREMENTS
22.5" width × 72.5" length, not including optional fringe

YARN
Wool of the Andes™ (worsted weight, 100% Peruvian Highland Wool; 110 yards/50g): Mineral Heather 25636, 14 skeins (add 1 skein for optional fringe)

NEEDLES
US 7 (4.5mm) straight or circular needles, or size to obtain gauge

NOTIONS
Yarn Needle
Stitch Markers
Cable Needle
Crochet Hook for Optional Fringe

GAUGE
1 repeat of Kells Chart center panel = 7.25" wide and 6" tall, blocked

For pattern support, contact knittingontheneedles@gmail.com

Kells Wrap

Notes:
The Kells Wrap is inspired by one of Ireland's finest national treasures, the famous ninth-century manuscript, the *Book of Kells*. Its intricate, intertwining cables draw their shape from the delicate illustrations and illuminated letters that decorate the pages of this historic document.

This generous wrap is worked flat in a single piece from one short end to the other. After binding off, optional fringe is attached using a crochet hook. Cable pattern is charted only.

Chart is worked flat; read RS rows (odd numbers) from right to left, and WS rows (even numbers) from left to right.

DIRECTIONS

Beginning Edge
Loosely CO 120 sts.
Knit three rows.

Body
Setup Row (WS): K4, M1, K2, P4, (K2, M1) two times, K2, P2, K1, M1, K1, P2, PM, *P2, K1, M1, K1, (P2, K2, M1, K2, M1, K2, P2) three times, K1, M1, K1, P2, PM; rep from * once more, P2, K1, M1, K1, P2, (K2, M1) two times, K2, P4, K2, M1, K4. 144 sts.

Cont working back and forth following Kells Chart, repeating center outlined sts (sts 27-72) two times; Ms should align with edges of outlined section. Note: on Rows 3, 15, 27, and 39, Ms will fall within a cable. Remove M when you get to this point, work cable crossing, then replace M in center of completed cable.

Cont as established until you have worked 12 reps of Kells Chart. Work Row 1 of Kells Chart once more.

Ending Edge
Ending Row (WS): K4, K2tog, K6, SSK, K2, K2tog, K4, K2tog, K2, remove M *K2, SSK, K1, (K3, SSK, K2, K2tog, K3) three times, K1, K2tog, K2, remove M; rep from * once more, K2, SSK, K4, SSK, K2, K2tog, K6, SSK, K4. 120 sts.
Knit one row.
BO loosely.

Finishing
Weave in ends, wash, and block to measurements.

Optional Fringe
After blocking, cut 12" lengths of yarn and arrange them in 120 bundles of 3 pieces. Starting at one corner of short edge, fold a bundle in half and use crochet hook to pull fold through, creating a loop; then pull ends through loop. Cont attaching fringe in every other BO or CO st across both short edges of wrap.

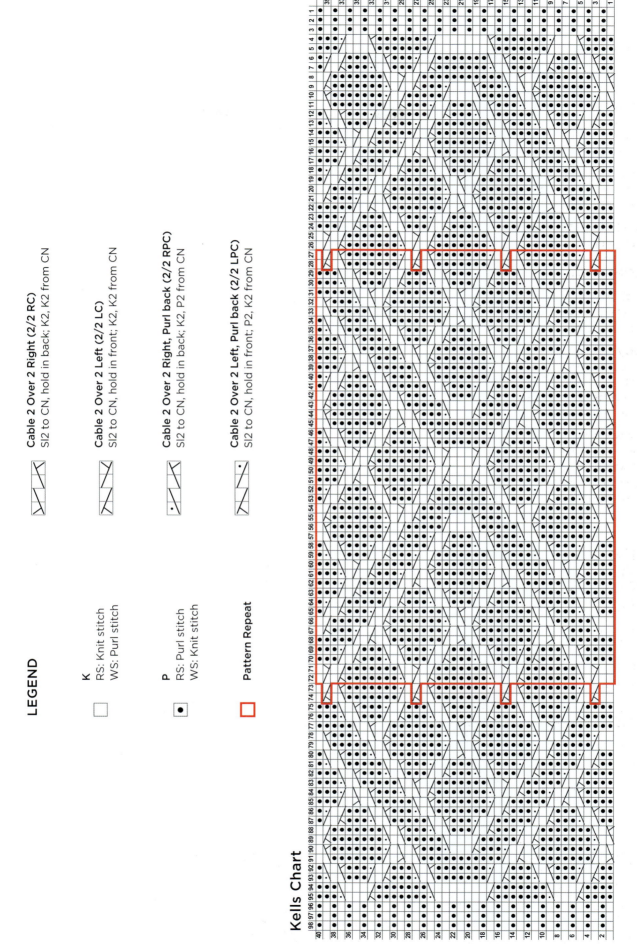

Kells Chart

KNOTS & CHAINS PULLOVER

by Sandi Rosner

FINISHED MEASUREMENTS
32 (36, 40, 44, 48, 52)" finished bust circumference; meant to be worn with 2" positive ease
Sample is 36" size; model is 34" bust

YARN
Wool of the Andes™ (sport weight, 100% Peruvian Highland Wool; 137 yards/50g): MC Pampas Heather 25653, 8 (9, 10, 11, 13, 14) skeins; CC Oyster Heather 25276, 1 (1, 1, 2, 2, 2) skeins

NEEDLES
US 3 (3.25mm) 16" and 32" circular needles, and DPNs or two 24" circular needles for two circulars technique or 32" or longer circular needles for Magic Loop technique, or size to obtain Stockinette Stitch gauge

US 4 (3.5mm) 16", 24", and 32" circular needles, and DPNs or two 24" circular needles for two circulars technique or 32" or longer circular needles for Magic Loop technique, or size to obtain gauge

NOTIONS
Yarn Needle
Stitch Markers
Scrap Yarn or Stitch Holder

GAUGE
24 sts and 30 rnds = 4" in Stranded Stockinette Stitch in the round on larger needles, blocked
24 sts and 30 rnds = 4" in Stockinette Stitch in the round on larger needles, blocked

For pattern support, contact rosnersandi@gmail.com

Knots & Chains Pullover

Notes:

The sinuous lines of traditional Celtic designs are a gift to the knitter. This pullover features two chain motifs framing a row of Celtic love knots, which are formed with two entwined hearts.

The Knots & Chains Pullover is worked in one piece from the top down, with folded hems at the neck, cuffs, and lower edge. The smaller chain motif is echoed on the sleeves.

The design on the yoke and the sleeves is worked using the stranded colorwork technique. Carry the color not in use loosely along the wrong side of the work.

Charts are worked in the round; read each chart row from right to left as a RS row.

DIRECTIONS

Collar

Using MC and smaller size 16" circular needles, loosely CO 126 (126, 132, 138, 144, 150) sts. PM for BOR, being careful not to twist sts.
Rnds 1-10: K all.
Rnd 11, Turning Ridge: P all.
Change to larger size 16" circular needles.
Rnds 12-21: K all.

Raise Back Neck with Short Rows

Short Row 1: K33 (33, 30, 31, 28, 31), W&T.
Short Row 2: Sl1, P66 (66, 60, 62, 56, 62), W&T.
Short Row 3: Sl1, K to wrapped st, K wrap tog with st, K5, W&T.
Short Row 4: Sl1, P to wrapped st, P wrap tog with st, P5, W&T.
Rep Short Rows 3-4 1 (1, 2, 2, 3, 3) more times.
Last Short Row: Sl1, K to BOR.

Yoke

Rnd 1: K all, knitting wraps tog with wrapped sts as you come to them.
Rnd 2, Inc Rnd: *K4 (4, 3, 3, 3, 3), M1; rep from * to last 2 (2, 0, 0, 0, 0) sts, K2 (2, 0, 0, 0, 0). 157 (157, 176, 184, 192, 200) sts.
Change to larger size 24" circular needles.
Knit 1 (1, 4, 4, 6, 6) rnds even.
Inc Rnd: *K52 (52, 11, 23, 6, 8), M1; rep from * to last 1 (1, 0, 0, 0, 8) sts, K1 (1, 0, 0, 0, 8). 160 (160, 192, 192, 224, 224) sts.
Remove BOR M, K8, PM for new BOR. BOR is to the right of the center back as worn.

Work all rnds of Chart A. Chart is worked 10 (10, 12, 12, 14, 14) times across each rnd.
Next Rnd: With MC, K all.
Inc Rnd: K3, M1, (K4, M1) to last st, K1. 200 (200, 240, 240, 280, 280) sts.
Change to larger size 32" circular needles.

Work all rnds of Chart B. Chart is worked 10 (10, 12, 12, 14, 14) times across each rnd. Note incs in Rnd 2 of Chart B. After Rnd 2 of Chart B is complete, 220 (220, 264, 264, 308, 308) sts.

Work all rnds of Chart C. Chart is worked 10 (10, 12, 12, 14, 14) times across each rnd. Note incs in Rnds 1 and 4 of Chart C. After Rnd 1 of Chart C is complete, 280 (280, 336, 336, 392, 392) sts. After Rnd 4 of Chart C is complete, 300 (300, 360, 360, 420, 420) sts.
Break CC.

Next Rnd: With MC, K all.
Inc Rnd: *K25 (7, 25, 7, 35, 10), M1; rep from * to last 0 (20, 10, 24, 0, 0) sts, K0 (20, 10, 24, 0, 0). 312 (340, 374, 408, 432, 462) sts.
Knit 1 (3, 2, 6, 6, 9) rnds even.

Divide Body & Sleeves

Next Rnd: K27 (32, 37, 42, 47, 52) sts for Right Back, place next 66 (70, 77, 84, 86, 91) sts on scrap yarn or st holder for Right Sleeve, CO 6 (8, 10, 12, 14, 16) sts for underarm, K90 (100, 110, 120, 130, 140) sts for Front, place next 66 (70, 77, 84, 86, 91) sts on scrap yarn or st holder for Left Sleeve, CO 6 (8, 10, 12, 14, 16) sts for underarm, K63 (68, 73, 78, 83, 88) sts to end, PM for BOR. 192 (216, 240, 264, 288, 312) sts for Body.

Body

WE in St st until Body measures 16.25 (16.5, 16.5, 17, 17.5, 18)" from underarm.
Change to smaller size 32" circular needles.
Next Rnd, Turning Ridge: P all.
Knit ten rnds.
BO loosely.

Sleeves (work two the same)

Sl sleeves sts to larger size needles in preferred style for small circumference knitting in the rnd. Join yarn at center of underarm CO edge.
Rnd 1: PU and K 3 (4, 5, 6, 7, 8) sts along underarm edge, K66 (70, 77, 84, 86, 91) sleeve sts from holder, PU and K 3 (4, 5, 6, 7, 8) sts along underarm edge. PM for BOR. 72 (78, 87, 96, 100, 107) sts.
Knit four rnds.
Dec Rnd: K1, SSK, K to last 3 sts, K2tog, K1. 2 sts dec.
Cont in St st, rep Dec Rnd every 25 (16, 9, 7, 11, 8) rnds 3 (6, 10, 15, 9, 12) more times. 64 (64, 65, 64, 80, 81) sts.

WE in St st until sleeve measures 16", or 2" shorter than desired length.

Sizes 40" & 52" Only
Dec Rnd: K1, SSK, K to end. 1 st dec. 64 (80) sts.

All Sizes
Work all rnds of Chart A. Chart is worked 4 (4, 4, 4, 5, 5) times across each rnd.

46   Knots & Chains Pullover

Knit five rnds.

Change to smaller size needles in preferred style for small circumference knitting in the rnd.

Next Rnd, Turning Ridge: P all.

Knit ten rnds.

BO loosely.

Finishing

Weave in ends. Close up any little gaps at the underarms.

Fold hems under at collar, cuffs, and lower edge to WS at Turning Ridge. Sew in place, taking care to keep the stitching loose.

Wash and block to diagram.

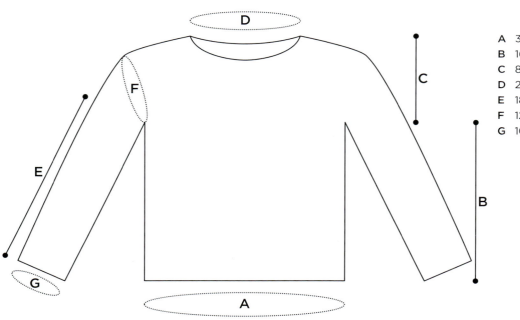

A 32 (36, 40, 44, 48, 52)"
B 16.25 (16.5, 16.5, 17, 17.5, 18)"
C 8.5 (8.75, 9, 9.5, 9.75, 10.25)"
D 21 (21, 22, 23, 24, 25)"
E 18"
F 12 (13, 14.5, 16, 16.75, 17.75)"
G 10.75 (10.75, 10.75, 10.75, 13.25, 13.25)"

LEGEND

- ■ Main Color
- □ Contrasting Color 1
- ■ No Stitch — Placeholder—no stitch made
- □ Knit Stitch
- M M1 — Make 1 stitch

Chart A

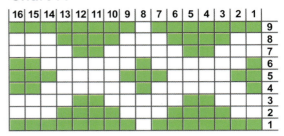

Chart B

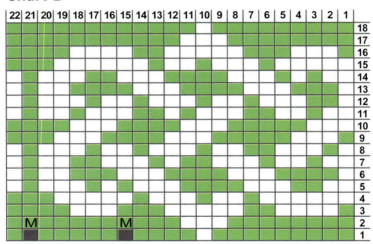

Chart C

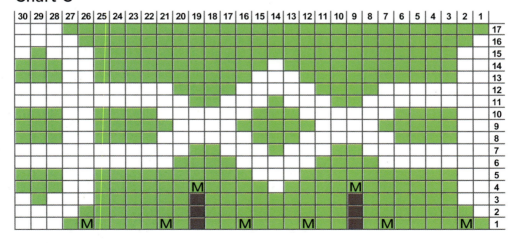

48 Knots & Chains Pullover

LINDISFARNE PONCHO

by Bridget Pupillo

FINISHED MEASUREMENTS
Two panels measuring 16 (20, 24)" × 23 (30, 37)"; to fit up to 30 (32-44, 46-58)" bust circumference
Sample is to fit 32-44"; model is 34" bust

YARN
Simply Wool™ (worsted weight, 100% Eco Wool; 218 yards/100g): Winnie 27470, 3 (5, 8) hanks

NEEDLES
US 7 (4.5mm) straight or circular needles, or size to obtain gauge

NOTIONS
Yarn Needle
Stitch Markers
Cable Needle
Scrap Yarn or Stitch Holder
1 (2, 2) 0.75" Decorative Buttons

GAUGE
18 sts and 32 rows = 4" in Chart 1 pattern, blocked
28 sts and 29 rows = 4" in Chart 4 pattern, blocked

For pattern support, contact brigittissima@gmail.com

Lindisfarne Poncho

Notes:
Inspired by the intricate Celtic illuminations of the Lindisfarne Gospels, the Aran cables on this poncho swirl and intertwine to create a beautiful flowing design. Lindisfarne is a perfect sampler of advanced cable knitting motifs.

The Lindisfarne Poncho is constructed from two rectangular panels, knitted flat and sewn together with a center neck opening. A variety of cable patterns are worked across the width of each panel. Stitches are then picked up along the neckline and knitted flat with buttonhole(s) along the neckband edge.

Charts are worked flat; read RS rows (odd numbers) from right to left, and WS rows (even numbers) from left to right.

2/2 LC (cable 2 over 2 left)
Sl2 to CN, hold in front; K2, K2 from CN.

2/2 RC (cable 2 over 2 right)
Sl2 to CN, hold in back; K2, K2 from CN.

2/1 LPC (cable 2 over 1 left, purl back)
Sl2 to CN, hold in front; P1, K2 from CN.

2/1 RPC (cable 2 over 1 right, purl back)
Sl1 to CN, hold in back; K2, P1 from CN.

2/2 LPC (cable 2 over 2 left, purl back)
Sl2 to CN, hold in front; P2, K2 from CN.

2/2 RPC (cable 2 over 2 right, purl back)
Sl2 to CN, hold in back; K2, P2 from CN.

Chart 1 (flat over a multiple of 4 sts plus 3)
Row 1 (RS): K across.
Row 2 (WS): K3, (P1, K3) to end.
Row 3: K across.
Row 4: K3, (P1, K3) to end.
Row 5: K across.
Row 6: K1, P1, K1, (K2, P1, K1) to end.
Row 7: K across.
Row 8: K1, P1, K1, (K2, P1, K1) to end.
Rep Rows 1-8 for pattern.

Chart 2 (flat over 14 sts)
Row 1 (RS): P2, K2, (2/2 LC) two times, P2.
Row 2 (WS): K2, P10, K2.
Row 3: P2, (2/2 RC) two times, K2, P2.
Row 4: K2, P10, K2.
Rep Rows 1-4 for pattern.

Chart 3 (flat over 12 sts)
Row 1 (RS): 2/2 LPC, P2, K4, P2.
Row 2 (WS): K2, P4, K2, P2, K2.
Row 3: P2, (2/2 LC) two times, P2.
Row 4: K2, P2, K2, P4, K2.
Row 5: 2/2 RPC, 2/2 LPC, K2, P2.
Row 6: K2, P4, K4, P2.
Row 7: K2, P4, 2/2 LC, P2.
Row 8: K2, P4, K4, P2.
Rep Rows 1-8 for pattern.

Chart 4 (flat over an even number of sts)
Row 1 (RS): K2, P12, K4, P12, K2.
Row 2 (WS): P2, K12, P4, K12, P2.
Row 3: K2, P5, M1L, M1R, P2, M1L, M1R, P5, 2/2 LC, P5, M1L, M1R, P2, M1L, M1R, P5, K2. 8 sts inc.
Row 4: P2, K5, P2, K2, P2, K5, P4, K5, P2, K2, P2, K5, P2.
Row 5: K2, P5, K1, M1L, M1R, K1, P2, K1, M1L, M1R, K1, P5, K4, P5, K1, M1L, M1R, K1, P2, K1, M1L, M1R, K1, P5, K2. 8 sts inc.
Row 6: P2, K4, P5, K2, P5, K4, P4, K4, P5, K2, P5, K4, P2.
Row 7: K2, P4, 2/1 RPC, K2, P2, K2, 2/1 LPC, P4, 2/2 LC, P4, 2/1 RPC, K2, P2, K2, 2/1 LPC, P4, K2.
Row 8: P2, K4, P2, K1, P2, K2, P2, K1, P2, K4, P4, K4, P2, K1, P2, K2, P2, K1, P2, K4, P2.
Row 9: 2/2 LPC, 2/2 RPC, P1, K2, P2, K2, P1, (2/2 LPC, 2/2 RPC) two times, P1, K2, P2, K2, P1, 2/2 LPC, 2/2 RPC.
Row 10: K2, P4, K3, P2, K2, P2, K3, P4, K4, P4, K3, P2, K2, P2, K3, P4, K2.
Row 11: P2, 2/2 RC, P3, K2, P2, K2, P3, 2/2 RC, P4, 2/2 RC, P3, K2, P2, K2, P3, 2/2 RC, P2.
Row 12: K2, P4, K3, P2, K2, P2, K3, P4, K4, P4, K3, P2, K2, P2, K3, P4, K2.
Row 13: 2/2 RPC, 2/2 LPC, 2/1 RPC, P2, 2/1 LPC, (2/2 RPC, 2/2 LPC) two times, 2/1 RPC, P2, 2/1 LPC, 2/2 RPC, 2/2 LPC.
Row 14: P2, (K4, P4) five times, K4, P2.
Row 15: K2, (P4, 2/2 LC) five times, P4, K2.
Row 16: P2, (K4, P4) five times, K4, P2.
Row 17: (2/2 LPC, 2/2 RPC) six times.
Row 18: K2, P4, K4, P4, K4, P4, K4, P4, K4, P4, K2.
Row 19: P2, 2/2 RC, P4, 2/2 RC, P4, 2/2 RC, P4, 2/2 RC, P4, 2/2 RC, P4, 2/2 RC, P2.
Row 20: K2, P4, K4, P4, K4, P4, K4, P4, K4, P4, K2.
Row 21: 2/2 RPC, 2/2 LPC, 2/2 RPC, 2/2 LPC, 2/2 RPC, 2/2 LPC, 2/2 RPC, 2/2 LPC, 2/2 RPC, 2/2 LPC, 2/2 RPC, 2/2 LPC.
Row 22: P2, (K4, P4) five times, K4, P2.
Row 23: K2, (P4, 2/2 LC) five times, P4, K2.
Row 24: P2, (K4, P4) five times, K4, P2.
Row 25: 2/2 LPC, 2/2 RPC, 2/1 LPC, P2, 2/1 RPC, (2/2 LPC, 2/2 RPC) two times, 2/1 LPC, P2, 2/1 RPC, 2/2 LPC, 2/2 RPC.
Row 26: K2, P4, K3, P2, K2, P2, K3, P4, K4, P4, K3, P2, K2, P2, K3, P4, K2.
Row 27: P2, 2/2 RC, P3, K2, P2, K2, P3, 2/2 RC, P4, 2/2 RC, P3, K2, P2, K2, P3, 2/2 RC, P2.

Row 28: K2, P4, K3, P2, K2, P2, K3, P4, K4, P4, K3, P2, K2, P2, K3, P4, K2.
Row 29: 2/2 RPC, 2/2 LPC, P1, K2, P2, K2, P1, (2/2 RPC, 2/2 LPC) two times, P1, K2, P2, K2, P1, 2/2 RPC, 2/2 LPC.
Row 30: P2, K4, P2, K1, P2, K2, P2, K1, P2, K4, P4, K4, P2, K1, P2, K2, P2, K1, P2, K4, P2.
Row 31: K2, P4, 2/1 LPC, K2, P2, K2, 2/1 RPC, P4, K4, P4, 2/1 LPC, K2, P2, K2, 2/1 RPC, P4, K2.
Row 32: P2, K5, P4, K2, P4, K5, P4, K5, P4, K2, P4, K5, P2.
Row 33: K2, P5, SSK, K2tog, P2, SSK, K2tog, P5, 2/2 LC, P5, SSK, K2tog, P2, SSK, K2tog, P5, K2. 8 sts dec.
Row 34: P2, K4, K2tog, SSK, K2tog, SSK, K4, P4, K4, K2tog, SSK, K2tog, SSK, K4, P2. 8 sts dec.
Row 35: 2/2 LPC, P8, 2/2 RPC, 2/2 LPC, P8, 2/2 RPC.
Row 36: K2, P2, K8, P2, K4, P2, K8, P2, K2.
Row 37: P2, 2/2 LPC, P4, 2/2 RPC, P4, 2/2 LPC, P4, 2/2 RPC, P2.
Row 38: K4, P2, K4, P2, K8, P2, K4, P2, K4.
Row 39: P4, 2/2 LPC, 2/2 RPC, P8, 2/2 LPC, 2/2 RPC, P4.
Row 40: K6, P4, K12, P4, K6.
Row 41: P6, 2/2 RC, P12, 2/2 RC, P6.
Row 42: K6, P4, K12, P4, K6.
Row 43: P4, 2/2 RPC, 2/2 LPC, P8, 2/2 RPC, 2/2 LPC, P4.
Row 44: K4, P2, K4, P2, K8, P2, K4, P2, K4.
Row 45: P2, 2/2 RPC, P4, 2/2 LPC, P4, 2/2 RPC, P4, 2/2 LPC, P2.
Row 46: K2, P2, K8, P2, K4, P2, K8, P2, K2.
Row 47: 2/2 RPC, P8, 2/2 LPC, 2/2 RPC, P8, 2/2 LPC.
Row 48: P2, K12, P4, K12, P2.
Row 49: K2, P12, K4, P12, K2.
Row 50: P2, K12, P4, K12, P2.
Row 51: K2, P5, M1L, M1R, P2, M1L, M1R, P5, 2/2 LC, P5, M1L, M1R, P2, M1L, M1R, P5, K2. 8 sts inc.
Row 52: P2, K5, P2, K2, P2, K5, P4, K5, P2, K2, P2, K5, P2.
Row 53: K2, P5, K1, M1L, M1R, K1, P2, K1, M1L, M1R, K1, P5, K4, P5, K1, M1L, M1R, K1, P2, K1, M1L, M1R, K1, P5, K2. 8 sts inc.
Row 54: P2, K4, P5, K2, P5, K4, P4, K4, P5, K2, P5, K4, P2.
Row 55: K2, P4, 2/1 RPC, K2, P2, K2, 2/1 LPC, P4, 2/2 LC, P4, 2/1 RPC, K2, P2, K2, 2/1 LPC, P4, K2.
Row 56: P2, K4, P2, K1, P2, K2, P2, K1, P2, K4, P4, K4, P2, K1, P2, K2, P2, K1, P2, K4, P2.
Row 57: 2/2 LPC, 2/2 RPC, P1, K2, P2, K2, P1, (2/2 LPC, 2/2 RPC) two times, P1, K2, P2, K2, P1, 2/2 LPC, 2/2 RPC.
Row 58: K2, P4, K3, P2, K2, P2, K3, P4, K4, P4, K3, P2, K2, P2, K3, P4, K2.
Row 59: P2, 2/2 RC, P3, K2, P2, K2, P3, 2/2 RC, P4, 2/2 RC, P3, K2, P2, K2, P3, 2/2 RC, P2.
Row 60: K2, P4, K3, P2, K2, P2, K3, P4, K4, P4, K3, P2, K2, P2, K3, P4, K2.
Row 61: 2/2 RPC, 2/2 LPC, 2/1 RPC, P2, 2/1 LPC, (2/2 RPC, 2/2 LPC) two times, 2/1 RPC, P2, 2/1 LPC, 2/2 RPC, 2/2 LPC.
Row 62: P2, (K4, P4) five times, K4, P2.
Row 63: K2, (P4, 2/2 LC) five times, P4, K2.
Row 64: P2, (K4, P4) five times, K4, P2.
Row 65: (2/2 LPC, 2/2 RPC) six times.
Row 66: K2, (P4, K4) five times, P4, K2.
Row 67: P2, (2/2 RC, P4) five times, 2/2 RC, P2

Row 68: K2, (P4, K4) five times, P4, K2.
Row 69: (2/2 RPC, 2/2 LPC) six times.
Row 70: P2, (K4, P4) five times, K4, P2.
Row 71: K2, (P4, 2/2 LC) five times, P4, K2.
Row 72: P2, (K4, P4) five times, K4, P2.
Row 73: 2/2 LPC, 2/2 RPC, 2/1 LPC, P2, 2/1 RPC, (2/2 LPC, 2/2 RPC) two times, 2/1 LPC, P2, 2/1 RPC, 2/2 LPC, 2/2 RPC.
Row 74: K2, P4, K3, P2, K2, P2, K3, P4, K4, P4, K3, P2, K2, P2, K3, P4, K2.
Row 75: P2, 2/2 RC, P3, K2, P2, K2, P3, 2/2 RC, P4, 2/2 RC, P3, K2, P2, K2, P3, 2/2 RC, P2.
Row 76: K2, P4, K3, P2, K2, P2, K3, P4, K4, P4, K3, P2, K2, P2, K3, P4, K2.
Row 77: 2/2 RPC, 2/2 LPC, P1, K2, P2, K2, P1, 2/2 RPC, 2/2 LPC, 2/2 RPC, 2/2 LPC, P1, K2, P2, K2, P1, 2/2 RPC, 2/2 LPC.
Row 78: P2, K4, P2, K1, P2, K2, P2, K1, P2, K4, P4, K4, P2, K1, P2, K2, P2, K1, P2, K4, P2.
Row 79: K2, P4, 2/1 LPC, K2, P2, K2, 2/1 RPC, P4, K4, P4, 2/1 LPC, K2, P2, K2, 2/1 RPC, P4, K2.
Row 80: P2, K5, P4, K2, P4, K5, P4, K5, P4, K2, P4, K5, P2.
Row 81: K2, P5, SSK, K2tog, P2, SSK, K2tog, P5, 2/2 LC, P5, SSK, K2tog, P2, SSK, K2tog, P5, K2. 8 sts dec.
Row 82: P2, K4, K2tog, SSK, K2tog, SSK, K4, P4, K4, K2tog, SSK, K2tog, SSK, K4, P2. 8 sts dec.
Row 83: K2, P12, K4, P12, K2.
Row 84: P2, K12, P4, K12, P2.
Work Rows 1-32 once, then work Rows 33-80 2 (3, 4) times, then work Rows 81-84 once.

Chart 5 (flat over 12 sts)
Row 1 (RS): P2, K4, P2, 2/2 RPC.
Row 2 (WS): K2, P2, K2, P4, K2.
Row 3: P2, (2/2 RC) two times, P2.
Row 4: K2, P4, K2, P2, K2.
Row 5: P2, K2, 2/2 RPC, 2/2 LPC.
Row 6: P2, K4, P4, K2.
Row 7: P2, 2/2 RC, P4, K2.
Row 8: P2, K4, P4, K2.
Rep Rows 1-8 for pattern.

Chart 6 (flat over a multiple of 6 sts plus 4)
Row 1 (RS): K4, (P2, K4) to end.
Row 2 (WS): P4, (K2, P4) to end.
Row 3: 2/2 LC, (P2, 2/2 LC) to end.
Row 4: P4, (K2, P4) to end.
Rep Rows 1-4 for pattern.

DIRECTIONS

Panel (make two the same)
CO 71 (91, 107) sts.
Row 1 (WS): K across.
Row 2 (RS): Using chart or written instructions, work Row 1 of Chart 1.
Rep Chart 1 until panel measures 2.25 (2.5, 2.75)", ending on a RS row.

Bust Circumference Size 30" Only
Inc Row (WS): Work as established for 7 sts, PM, K7, M1, K6, PM, K16, M1, K15, PM, K7, M1, K6, PM, work as established over last 7 sts. 74 sts.
Cable Setup Row (RS): Work as established for 7 sts, SM, work Row 1 of Chart 2, SM, work Row 1 of Chart 4, SM, work Row 1 of Chart 2, SM, work as established over last 7 sts.

Bust Circumference Sizes - (32-44, 46-58)" Only
Inc Row (WS): Work as established for - (7, 15) sts, PM, K7, M1, K6, PM, K6, M1, K5, PM, (K7, M1) two times, K8, M1, K7, PM, K6, M1, K5, PM, K7, M1, K6, PM, work as established over last - (7, 15) sts. (98, 114) sts.
Cable Setup Row (RS): Work as established for - (7, 15) sts, SM, work Row 1 of Chart 2, SM, work Row 1 of Chart 3, SM, work Row 1 of Chart 4, SM, work Row 1 of Chart 5, SM, work Row 1 of Chart 2, SM, work as established over last - (7, 15) sts.

Resume All Sizes
Cont working all rows of each chart in order established in Cable Setup Row. Work Rows 1-32 of Chart 4, then work Rows 33-80 two (three, four) times, then work Rows 81-84.

Next Row (RS): Work as established for 7 (7, 15) sts, remove M, work Chart 1 to last M decreasing 3 (7, 7) sts evenly and removing all Ms, work Chart 1 over last 7 (7, 15) sts. 71 (91, 107) sts.

Rep Chart 1 until panel measures 23 (30, 37)" in length, ending with a WS row.
BO all sts in pattern.

Assembling
Weave in all ends, wash, and block both panels to diagram before continuing. With RSs tog and WSs facing out, pin CO edge of first panel to side edge of second panel as shown in diagram. Sew in place. With RSs tog and WSs facing out, pin CO edge of second panel to side edge of first panel as shown in diagram. Sew in place.

Neckband
Hold poncho with two long points at center back and front. With RS facing, PU and K 84 (110, 134) sts along neck opening, beginning and ending at front seam and working from right to left side of opening. Turn to work flat.
Row 1 (WS): K across.
Neckband Setup Row (RS): Work Row 1 of Chart 1 for 7 (11, 11) sts, PM, work Row 1 of Chart 6 for 70 (88, 112) sts, PM, work Row 1 of Chart 1 for 7 (11, 11) sts.
Work next three rows in established pattern.
Buttonhole Row (RS): K3 (5, 5), YO, K2tog, K2 (4, 4), work to end in established pattern.

Bust Circumference Size 30" Only
Work five rows in established pattern.
BO all sts in pattern.

Bust Circumference Sizes - (32-44, 46-58)" Only
Work seven rows in established pattern.
Work Buttonhole Row once more.
Work five rows in established pattern.
BO all sts in pattern.

Finishing
Weave in all ends.
Overlap front edges of neckband and mark for button placement. Sew 1 (2, 2) button(s) as marked on neckband.

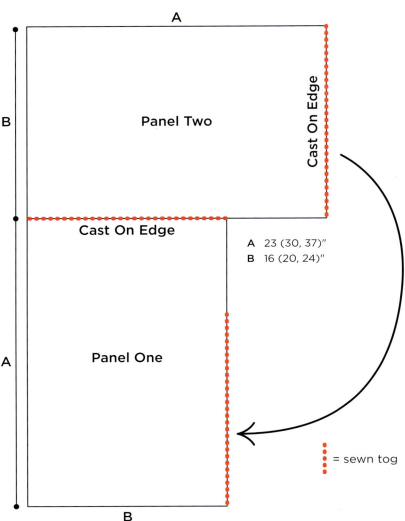

A 23 (30, 37)"
B 16 (20, 24)"

••• = sewn tog

LEGEND

- ■ **No Stitch** — Placeholder—no stitch made
- □ **K** — RS: Knit stitch / WS: Purl stitch
- • **P** — RS: Purl stitch / WS: Knit stitch
- ⁄ **K2tog** — Knit 2 stitches together as one stitch
- \ **SSK** — Slip, slip, knit slipped stitches together
- ⁄• **P2tog (K2tog on WS)** — WS: Knit 2 stitches together as one stitch
- •\ **P2tog TBL (SSK on WS)** — WS: Slip, slip, knit slipped stitches together
- [MR] **M1R** — Make 1 right-leaning stitch
- [ML] **M1L** — Make 1 left-leaning stitch
- **Cable 2 Over 2 Right (2/2 RC)** — Sl2 to CN, hold in back; K2, K2 from CN
- **Cable 2 Over 2 Left (2/2 LC)** — Sl2 to CN, hold in front; K2, K2 from CN
- **Cable 2 Over 2 Right, Purl back (2/2 RPC)** — Sl2 to CN, hold in back; K2, P2 from CN
- **Cable 2 Over 2 Left, Purl back (2/2 LPC)** — Sl2 to CN, hold in front; P2, K2 from CN
- **Cable 2 Over 1 Right, Purl back (2/1 RPC)** — Sl1 to CN, hold in back; K2, P1 from CN
- **Cable 2 Over 1 Left, Purl back (2/1 LPC)** — Sl2 to CN, hold in front; P1, K2 from CN
- ▭ **Pattern Repeat**

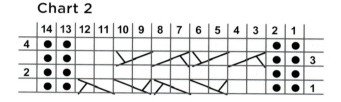

See next page for Chart 4.

Chart 4

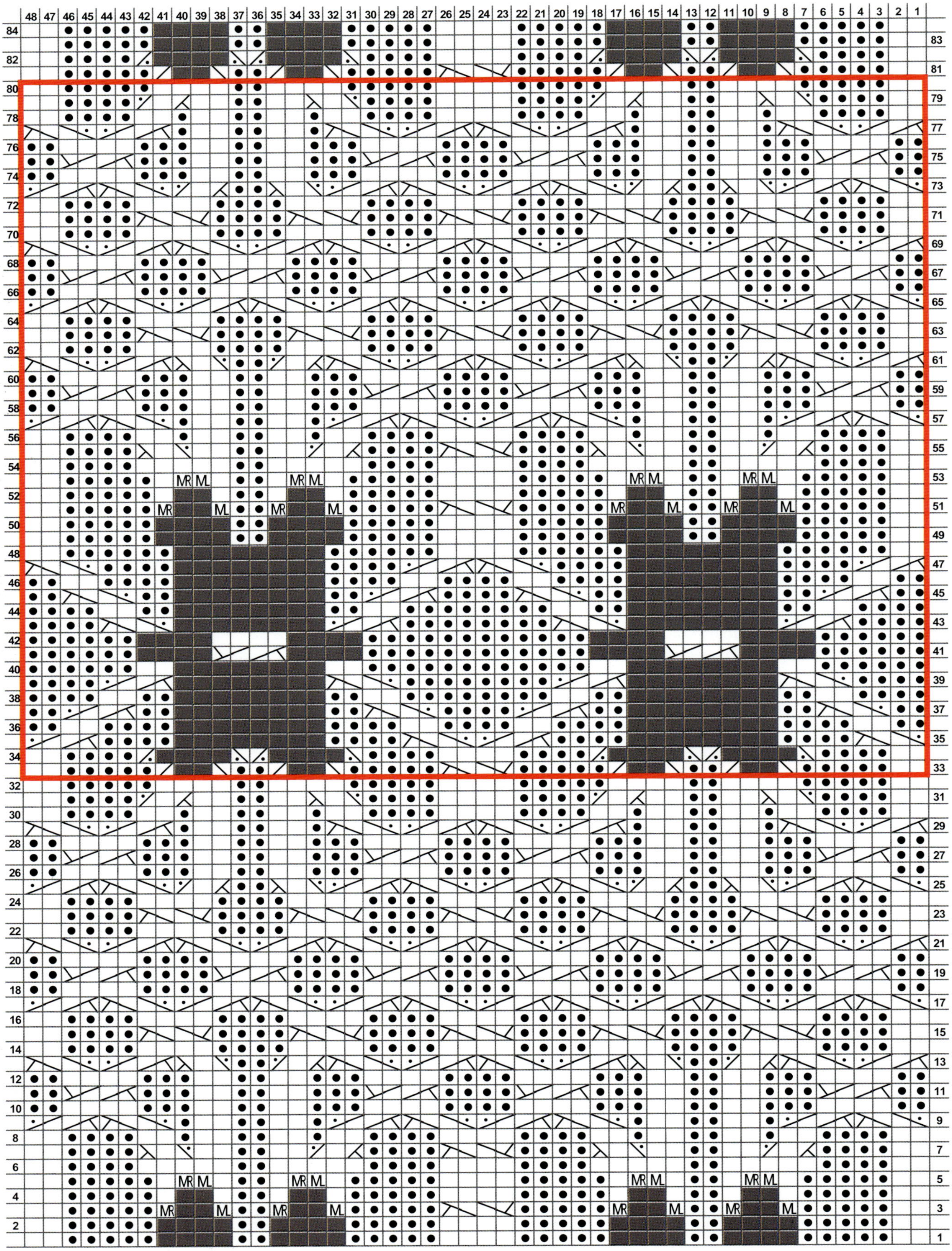

56 Lindisfarne Poncho

MORAG PULLOVER
by Elly Doyle

FINISHED MEASUREMENTS
35.25 (38.75, 40.25, 43.75, 47, 50.5, 53.75, 55.5, 59, 62.25)" finished bust circumference; meant to be worn with 2-4" positive ease
Sample is 38.75" size; model is 34" bust

YARN
Wool of the Andes™ (sport weight, 100% Peruvian Highland Wool; 137 yards/50g): Merlot Heather 25292, 8 (9, 9, 10, 10, 11, 12, 12, 13, 13) skeins

NEEDLES
US 7 (4.5mm) straight needles, or size to obtain gauge
US 4 (3.5mm) straight needles, or three sizes smaller than size used to obtain gauge

NOTIONS
Yarn Needle
Stitch Markers
Cable Needle
Scrap Yarn or Stitch Holders
Crochet Hook (in size similar to smaller needles)

GAUGE
19 sts and 27 rows = 4" in Stockinette Stitch, lightly blocked
Main Body Cable Chart (1 rep) = 5" wide, lightly blocked
Main Sleeve Cable Chart (1 rep) = 2.5" wide, lightly blocked

For pattern support, contact support@magpielly.co.uk

Morag Pullover

Notes:
Inspired by the early stone carvings found throughout Scotland, Morag echoes the flowing and interlocking braids that often feature on these intriguing relics.

Cables flow from hem and cuff ribbing up the body and sleeves; a saddle-shoulder enables the lines of the cable to merge at the corners and back of neckline. A plain back hastens the completion of what is sure to become a wardrobe staple. Sweater is knit flat and seamed.

Charts are worked flat; read RS rows (odd numbers) from right to left, and WS rows (even numbers) from left to right.

M1P (make 1 purl stitch)
Inserting LH needle from back to front, PU horizontal strand between st just worked and next st, and P into it.

DS (double stitch)
Work a Sl st as per German Short Row instructions.

Pass-Over Crochet Bind Off
Prepare both sets of live sts by slipping to needles. If using straights ensure points are pointing downwards, as you will be working upwards towards nape of neck. Sl first st on RH side to hook; Sl first st on LH to hook and draw through st already on hook. *Sl next st on RH needle to hook, and draw through st already on hook; Sl next st on LH needle to hook, and draw through st already on hook; rep from * until all sts are used—you will have one st left on hook. Draw through a tail from one side of the Shoulder Strap to secure. Weave in tail.

DIRECTIONS

Front
Using smaller needles, loosely CO 86 (94, 98, 106, 114, 122, 130, 134, 142, 150) sts.
Next Row (RS): P2, (2, 0, 0, 0, 0, 0, 2, 2, 2), work 2x2 Rib to end, ending K0 (0, 2, 2, 2, 2, 2, 0, 0, 0).
Work as established until piece measures 1.5 (1.5, 2, 2, 2, 2.5, 2.5, 2.5, 2.5)".

Change to larger needles.
Row 1 (RS): P2, M1P, P28 (32, 34, 38, 42, 46, 50, 52, 56, 60), PM, work Row 1 of Foundation Body Chart, PM, P to last 2 sts, M1P, P2. 90 (98, 102, 110, 118, 126, 134, 138, 146, 154) sts.
Row 2 (WS): K to M, work Row 2 of Foundation Body Chart, K to end.
Row 3: P to M, work Row 3 of Foundation Body Chart, P to end. 94 (102, 106, 114, 122, 130, 138, 142, 150, 158) sts.
Row 4: K to M, work Row 4 of Foundation Body Chart, K to end.
Row 5: P to M, work Row 7 of Main Body Chart, P to end.
Work as established, though Main Body Chart to Row 20, then rep Rows 1-20 until piece measures 19.25 (19, 18.5, 18.5, 18, 17.75, 17.75, 17.25, 17, 16.5)" or desired length to underarm, ending with a WS row.

Shape Underarm
Cont to rep Rows 1-20 of Main Body Chart while working through underarm shaping.
At beginning of next two rows, BO 0 (0, 0, 4, 6, 6, 6, 6, 8, 10) sts. 94 (102, 106, 106, 110, 118, 126, 130, 134, 138) sts.
At beginning of next two rows, BO 0 (0, 0, 0, 0, 0, 4, 4, 4, 6) sts. 94 (102, 106, 106, 110, 118, 118, 122, 126, 126) sts.
At beginning of next two rows, BO 3 sts. 88 (96, 100, 100, 104, 112, 112, 116, 120, 120) sts.
At beginning of next four rows, BO 2 sts. 80 (88, 92, 92, 96, 104, 104, 108, 112, 112) sts.
Row 1 (RS, Dec Row): SSP, work in pattern to last 2 sts, P2tog. 2 sts dec.
Row 2 (WS): WE as established.
Rep Rows 1-2 1 (3, 4, 2, 2, 5, 5, 5, 6, 6) more times. 76 (80, 82, 86, 90, 92, 92, 96, 98, 98) sts.

WE until piece measures approx 24" from CO edge, ending after Row 20 of chart. Move each M 5 sts outwards to sides of piece.

Divide for Neck
Work first six rows of Neckline chart, working across all sts as established: Rev St st outside Ms, chart between Ms. At Row 7 work to gap with working yarn, join second ball for use on other half of neckline.
Work through Neckline Chart using both balls of yarn; remove Ms on last row. 29 (31, 32, 34, 36, 37, 37, 39, 40, 40) sts each shoulder.

Left Front
Row 1 (RS): P to last 13 sts, K2tog, K1, P2, K2, P2, K2tog, K2. 27 (29, 30, 32, 34, 35, 35, 37, 38, 38) shoulder sts.
Row 2 (WS): P3, K2, P2, K2, P1, SSP, K to end. 26 (28, 29, 31, 33, 34, 34, 36, 37, 37) sts.
Row 3: P to last 12 sts, K2tog, K1, P2, K2, P2, K3. 1 st dec.
Row 4: P3, K2, P2, K2, P1, SSP, K to end. 1 st dec.
Rep Rows 3-4 1 (1, 1, 2, 2, 3, 3, 3, 3, 3) more times. 22 (24, 25, 25, 27, 26, 26, 28, 29, 29) sts.
Work Row 3 0 (0, 1, 1, 1, 0, 0, 0, 1, 1) time. 22 (24, 24, 24, 26, 26, 26, 28, 28, 28) sts.

WE until armhole measures 7.5 (8, 8.25, 8.75, 9, 9.5, 9.75, 10.25, 11, 11.5)", finishing after a WS row.

Left Shoulder Shaping
Using German Short Rows method, work short rows through Short Row 3 (3, 3, 3, 5, 5, 5, 7, 7, 7) then work Row 8.
Row 1 (RS): Work in pattern to end.
Short Row 2 (WS): Work to last 10 (12, 12, 12, 6, 6, 6, 4, 4, 4) sts, turn.
Short Row 3: DS, work in pattern to end.
Short Row 4: Work to last 0 (0, 0, 0, 7, 7, 7, 5, 5, 5) sts before DS, turn.
Short Row 5: DS, work in pattern to end.

Short Row 6: Work to last 0 (0, 0, 0, 0, 0, 5, 5, 5) sts before DS, turn.
Short Row 7: DS, work in pattern to end.
Row 8: Work in pattern 12 sts, BO remaining sts. Place live sts on holder.

Right Front

Row 1 (RS): K2, SSK, P2, K2, P2, K1, SSK, P to end. 27 (29, 30, 32, 34, 35, 35, 37, 38, 38) sts.
Row 2 (WS): K to last 12 sts, SSP, P1, K2, P2, K2, P3. 26 (28, 29, 31, 33, 34, 34, 36, 37, 37) sts.
Row 3: K3, P2, K2, P2, K1, SSK, P to end. 1 st dec.
Row 4: K to last 12 sts, SSP, P1, K2, P2, K2, P3. 1 st dec.
Rep Rows 3-4 1 (1, 1, 2, 2, 3, 3, 3, 3, 3) more times. 22 (24, 25, 25, 27, 26, 26, 28, 29, 29) sts.
Work Row 3 row 0 (0, 1, 1, 1, 0, 0, 0, 1, 1) time. 22 (24, 24, 24, 26, 26, 26, 28, 28, 28) sts.

WE until armhole measures 7.5 (8, 8.25, 8.75, 9, 9.5, 9.75, 10.25, 11, 11.5)", or matches Left Front, finishing after a WS row.

Right Shoulder Shaping

Using German Short Rows method, work short rows through Short Row 2 (2, 2, 2, 4, 4, 4, 6, 6, 6) then work Row 7.
Short Row 1 (RS): Work to last 10 (12, 12, 12, 6, 6, 6, 4, 4, 4) sts, turn.
Short Row 2 (WS): DS, work in pattern to end.
Short Row 3: Work to last 0 (0, 0, 0, 7, 7, 7, 5, 5, 5) sts before DS, turn.
Short Row 4: DS, work in pattern to end.
Short Row 5: Work to last 0 (0, 0, 0, 0, 0, 0, 5, 5, 5) sts before DS, turn.
Short Row 6: DS, work in pattern to end.
Row 7: Work in pattern 12 sts, BO remain sts. Place live sts on holder.

Back

Using smaller needles, CO 86 (94, 98, 106, 114, 122, 130, 134, 142, 150) sts.
Work Rib as for Front.

Change to larger needles.
Work Rev St st until piece measures 19.25 (19, 18.5, 18.5, 18, 17.75, 17.75, 17.25, 17, 16.5)" or matches Front length, ending with a WS row.

Shape Underarm

At beginning of next two rows, BO 0 (0, 0, 4, 6, 6, 6, 6, 8, 10) sts. 86 (94, 98, 98, 102, 110, 118, 122, 126, 130) sts.
At beginning of next two rows, BO 0 (0, 0, 0, 0, 0, 4, 4, 4, 6) sts. 86 (94, 98, 98, 102, 110, 110, 114, 118, 118) sts.
At beginning of next two rows, BO 3 sts. 80, (88, 92, 92, 96, 104, 204, 108, 112, 112) sts.
At beginning of next four rows, BO 2 sts. 72 (80, 84, 84, 88, 96, 96, 100, 104, 104) sts.

Row 1 (RS, Dec Row): SSP, work in pattern to last 2 sts, P2tog. 2 sts dec.
Row 2 (WS): WE as established.
Rep Rows 1-2 1 (3, 4, 2, 2, 5, 5, 5, 6, 6) more times. 68 (72, 74, 78, 82, 84, 84, 88, 90, 90) sts.

WE until piece measures the same as Front at start of Shoulder Shaping.
Neck and Shoulder shaping will now be worked AT THE SAME TIME.

(Pattern continues after charts.)

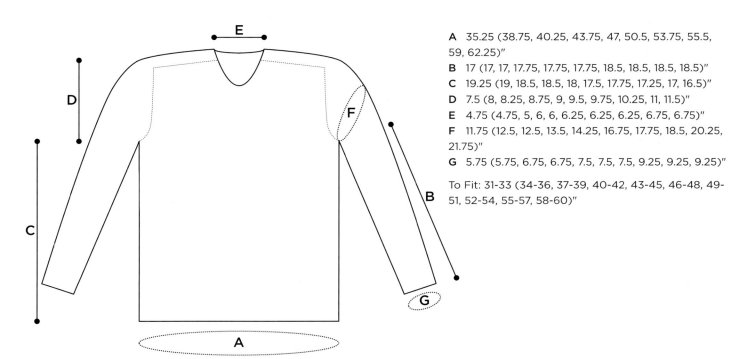

A 35.25 (38.75, 40.25, 43.75, 47, 50.5, 53.75, 55.5, 59, 62.25)"
B 17 (17, 17, 17.75, 17.75, 17.75, 18.5, 18.5, 18.5, 18.5)"
C 19.25 (19, 18.5, 18.5, 18, 17.5, 17.75, 17.25, 17, 16.5)"
D 7.5 (8, 8.25, 8.75, 9, 9.5, 9.75, 10.25, 11, 11.5)"
E 4.75 (4.75, 5, 6, 6, 6.25, 6.25, 6.25, 6.75, 6.75)"
F 11.75 (12.5, 12.5, 13.5, 14.25, 16.75, 17.75, 18.5, 20.25, 21.75)"
G 5.75 (5.75, 6.75, 6.75, 7.5, 7.5, 7.5, 9.25, 9.25, 9.25)"

To Fit: 31-33 (34-36, 37-39, 40-42, 43-45, 46-48, 49-51, 52-54, 55-57, 58-60)"

LEGEND

No Stitch
Placeholder—no stitch made

K
RS: Knit stitch
WS: Purl stitch

P
RS: Purl stitch
WS: Knit stitch

M1P
Make 1 purl stitch

Right Lifted Increase (RLI)
Knit into the right shoulder of the stitch below the stitch on the left-hand needle

Left Lifted Increase (LLI)
Knit into the left shoulder of the stitch two below the stitch on the right-hand needle

Right Lifted Purl Increase (RLPI)
Purl into the right shoulder of the stitch below the stitch on the left-hand needle

Left Lifted Purl Increase (LLPI)
Purl into the left shoulder of the stitch two below the stitch on the right-hand needle

K2tog
RS: Knit 2 stitches together as one stitch
WS: Purl 2 stitches together as one stitch

SSK
RS: Slip, slip, knit slipped stitches together
WS: Slip, slip, purl slipped stitches together

P2tog
RS: Purl 2 stitches together as one stitch
WS: Knit 2 stitches together as one stitch

SSP
RS: Slip, slip, purl slipped stitches together
WS: Slip, slip, knit slipped stitches together

Cable 2 Over 1 Right, Purl back (2/1 RPC)
Sl1 to CN, hold in back; K2, P1 from CN

Cable 2 Over 1 Left, Purl back (2/1 LPC)
Sl2 to CN, hold in front; P1, K2 from CN

Cable 2 Over 2 Right (2/2 RC)
Sl2 to CN, hold in back; K2, K2 from CN

Cable 2 Over 2 Left (2/2 LC)
Sl2 to CN, hold in front; K2, K2 from CN

Cable 2 Over 2 Right, Purl back (2/2 RPC)
Sl2 to CN, hold in back; K2, P2 from CN

Cable 2 Over 2 Left, Purl back (2/2 LPC)
Sl2 to CN, hold in front; P2, K2 from CN

Cable 2 Over 3 Right, Purl back (2/3 RPC)
Sl3 to CN, hold in back; K2, P3 from CN

Cable 2 Over 3 Left, Purl back (2/3 LPC)
Sl3 to CN, hold in front; P3, K2 from CN

Foundation Body Chart

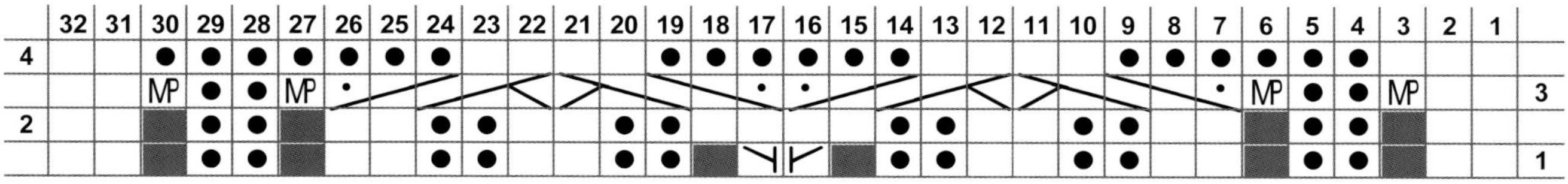

Main Body Chart

Neckline Chart

Foundation Sleeve Chart

Main Sleeve Chart

Strap Transition Chart

Right Back

Using German Short Rows method, work short rows through Short Row 3 (3, 3, 3, 5, 5, 5, 7, 7, 7) then work Row 8.

Short Row 1 (RS): P24 (26, 26, 26, 29, 29, 29, 32, 32, 32) sts, turn.
Short Row 2 (WS): DS, work in pattern to last 10 (12, 12, 12, 6, 6, 6, 4, 4, 4) sts, turn.
Short Row 3: DS, P to DS, turn.
Short Row 4: DS, P to 0 (0, 0, 0, 7, 7, 7, 5, 5, 5) sts before DS, turn.
Short Row 5: DS, P to DS, turn.
Short Row 6: DS, P to 0 (0, 0, 0, 0, 0, 0, 5, 5, 5) sts before DS, turn.
Short Row 7: DS, P until there are 23 (25, 25, 25, 27, 27, 29, 29, 29) sts on RH needle, turn.
Row 8: BO 23 (25, 25, 25, 27, 27, 27, 29, 29, 29) sts, break yarn. Sl the 1 (1, 1, 1, 2, 2, 2, 3, 3, 3) DSs and the next 21 (21, 23, 27, 26, 28, 28, 27, 29, 29) sts to a st holder.

Left Back

Using German Short Rows method, work short rows through Short Row 2 (2, 2, 2, 4, 4, 4, 6, 6, 6) then work Row 7.
With RS facing, join yarn 24 (26, 26, 26, 29, 29, 29, 32, 32, 32) sts in from LH side.
Short Row 1 (RS): P to last 10 (12, 12, 12, 6, 6, 6, 4, 4, 4) sts, turn.
Short Row 2 (WS): DS, K to DS, turn.
Short Row 3: DS, P to 0 (0, 0, 0, 7, 7, 7, 5, 5, 5) sts before DS, turn.
Short Row 4: DS, K to DS, turn.
Short Row 5: DS, P to 0 (0, 0, 0, 0, 0, 0, 5, 5, 5) sts before DS, turn.
Short Row 6: DS, K until there are 23 (25, 25, 25, 27, 27, 29, 29, 29) sts on RH needle, turn.
Row 7: BO 23 (25, 25, 25, 27, 27, 27, 29, 29, 29) sts, break yarn. BO remaining sts.

Sleeves (work two the same until Strap)

Using smaller needles CO 42 (42, 46, 46, 50, 50, 50, 58, 58, 58) sts.
Next Row (RS): P2 (2, 0, 0, 2, 2, 2, 2, 2, 2), work 2x2 Rib to end, ending K0 (0, 2, 2, 0, 0, 0, 0, 0, 0).
Work as established for 1.5 (1.5, 1.5, 2, 2, 2, 2, 2, 2, 2)", ending on a RS row.

Change to larger needles.
Next Row (WS): K8 (8, 10, 10, 12, 12, 12, 16, 16, 16), PM, work 2x2 Rib as set to last 8 (8, 10, 10, 12, 12, 12, 16, 16, 16) sts, PM, K to end.
Inc Row (RS): P2, M1P, P to M, SM, work Foundation Sleeve Chart, SM, P to last 2 sts, M1P, P2. 2 sts inc.

Work through Foundation Sleeve Chart once, then work reps of Main Sleeve Chart; AT THE SAME TIME, work shaping.
Rep Inc Row every 6 (6, 6, 5, 6, 4, 4, 4, 3, 3) rows 4 (12, 4, 10, 10, 10, 13, 15, 23, 29) more times, then every 7 (7, 7, 7, 5, 4, 5, 7, 8, 0) rows 9 (3, 9, 5, 5, 11, 10, 6, 2, 0) times. 70 (74, 74, 78, 82, 94, 98, 102, 110, 118) sts.

WE as established until piece measures 17 (17, 17, 17.75, 17.75, 17.75, 18.5, 18.5, 18.5, 18.5)" from CO edge, or desired length to underarm.

Shape Underarm

At beginning of next two rows, BO 0 (0, 0, 4, 6, 6, 6, 6, 8, 10) sts. 70 (74, 74, 70, 70, 82, 86, 90, 94, 98) sts.
At beginning of next two rows, BO 0 (0, 0, 0, 0, 0, 4, 4, 4, 6) sts. 70 (74, 74, 70, 70, 82, 78, 82, 86, 86) sts.
At beginning of next two rows, BO 3 sts. 64 (68, 68, 64, 64, 76, 72, 76, 80, 80) sts.
At beginning of next four rows, BO 2 sts. 56 (60, 60, 56, 56, 68, 64, 68, 72, 72) sts.

Row 1 (RS, Dec Row): SSP, work in pattern to last 2 sts, P2tog. 2 sts dec.
Row 2 (WS): WE as established.
Rep Rows 1-2 1 (3, 4, 2, 2, 5, 5, 5, 6, 6) more times. 52 (52, 50, 50, 50, 56, 52, 56, 58, 58) sts.
Dec Row (RS): SSP, work in pattern to last 2 sts, P2tog. 2 sts dec.
Work Dec Row every four rows a total of 0 (0, 2, 4, 3, 1, 3, 2, 3, 4) times, then every two rows 9 (9, 6, 4, 5, 10, 6, 9, 9, 8) times. 34 sts.

Row 1 (RS): SSP, work in pattern to last 2 sts, P2tog. 2 sts dec.
Row 2 (WS): P2tog, work in pattern to last 2 sts, SSP. 2 sts dec.
Rep Rows 1-2 once more. 26 sts.
The next time after Row 8 of Main Sleeve Chart is worked, switch to Strap Transition Chart.

Left Sleeve Strap

Work all rows of Strap Transition Chart once, then cont working 2x2 Rib as established by chart until strap measures length of BO sts across shoulders, ending after a WS row, measuring strap from end of dec shaping. Remove Ms. * Place held Left Neck sts on a needle ready to work (or work off holder) with RS facing.

Row 1 (RS): Working Sleeve Strap sts, Rib 13, place 13 sts just worked on st holder, Rib 10, SSK, P1, working Front sts K2tog, Rib 10. 23 sts.
Row 2 (WS): WE in Rib as set.
Row 3: Rib 10, CDD, Rib 10. 21 sts.
Row 4: WE in Rib as set.
Row 5: Rib to 1 st before CDD, CDD, Rib to end. 19 sts.
Row 6: Rib as set.
Rep Rows 5-6 until 1 st remains, fasten off.
Place remaining Strap sts on needles. Work 2x2 Rib until strap measures to center of Body. Work last row in St st; break yarn and place sts on st holder.

Right Sleeve Strap

Work as for Left until *, ending after a WS row (do not turn). Place Right Front sts on a needle ready to work (or work off holder) with WS facing, work across Front sts in Rib as set.

Row 1 (RS): Working across Front sts, Rib 10, SSK, working across Sleeve sts P1, K2tog, Rib 10. 2 sts dec.
Complete all other rows and steps as for Left.

Finishing

Weave in ends. Set in sleeves and sew straps to top of shoulders. Seam center back of shoulder straps by using Pass-Over Crochet Hook method, working upwards. Seam Body and Sleeves. Wash and block lightly to measurements.

NEVERN THROW

by Kath Andrews

FINISHED MEASUREMENTS
55.5 × 79.5"

YARN
Wool of the Andes™ Superwash (worsted weight, 100% Superwash Wool; 110 yards/50g): MC Noble Heather 26301, 28 skeins

and

Bare Wool of the Andes™ Superwash (worsted weight, 100% Superwash Wool; 220 yards/100g): CC Bare 26590, 8 hanks

NEEDLES
US 7 (4.5mm) straight or circular needles, or size to obtain gauge
US 4 (3.5mm) two 48" or 60" circular needles, or three sizes smaller than size used to obtain gauge

NOTIONS
Yarn Needle

GAUGE
20.5 sts and 20 rows = 4" in Stranded Stockinette Stitch, blocked (gauge is not crucial, but it will affect finished size and yardage requirements)

For pattern support, contact kath.andrews@btinternet.com

Nevern Throw

Notes:

The Great Cross of St Brynach (the Nevern Cross) is a 13-foot tall stone cross in Pembrokeshire, Wales, which dates from the tenth or eleventh century. It is decorated with many Celtic knots and patterns, and the scale and variety of designs are reflected in this large stranded colorwork throw.

Stranded squares are worked flat and separately, allowing Nevern Throw to be a project you can take with you, while the modular construction invites options for the positioning and use of motifs. Twenty-four squares of six different designs (in reality three, each with a reversed colorway twin) are bound together with a garter stitch border.

Twist the two yarns together at the very end of each row when working Stranded Stockinette Stitch (Rows 3-61 of every square).

As with all stranded colorwork, when there are more than five stitches of one color at a time, weave the yarn not in use to avoid long floats.

Charts are worked flat; read RS rows (odd numbers) from right to left, and WS rows (even numbers) from left to right.

DIRECTIONS

Squares 1, 3 & 5

Nevern Charts 1, 3 & 5 (make four of each)
With MC and larger needles, CO 65 sts using the Long Tail Cast On method.
Work Nevern Chart 1, 3, or 5, joining CC on Row 3 and breaking CC after Row 61.
After Row 63, BO P-wise on WS.

Squares 2, 4 & 6

Nevern Charts 2, 4 & 6 (make four of each)
With CC and larger needles, CO 65 sts using the Long Tail Cast On method.
Work Nevern Chart 2, 4, or 6, joining MC on Row 3 and breaking MC after Row 61.
After Row 63, BO P-wise on WS.

Making Up

Block each square to 12.75" wide × 12.5" high as you finish it, but do not weave in ends yet. Consider drawing the outline of the square onto a blocking board to reduce time spent measuring.

Horizontal Rows of Four Squares

Follow the diagram for the layout of the squares, and ensure they are all facing with the BO at the top as you join them.

Begin at the bottom of the diagram and work upwards, joining squares into six rows of four.

Horizontal Row 1
With RS facing, using MC and smaller circular needles, PU and K 63 sts up RH side of Square 2 (the leftmost bottom square).
Work 7 rows of Garter st, ending after a WS row. Break yarn, leaving sts on needle.
With RS facing, using MC and second smaller circular needles, PU and K 63 sts down LH side of Square 3.
Work 7 rows of Garter st as before, but do not break yarn.
Turn as if to work another row (RS facing) and place Square 2 in front of it with WS facing you. Using yarn from needle behind, join using a 3-Needle Bind Off.

Rep to join Square 4 to Square 3 and Square 1 to Square 4.

Rep this process for each Horizontal row.

Joining Rows of Squares Together

Take the bottom row of squares (Squares 2-3-4-1) and with RS facing, MC, and smaller circular needles, PU and K 64 sts from first BO edge (Square 1), *PU and K 8 sts across Garter st edge, PU and K 64 sts from next BO edge; rep from * to end. 280 sts.
Work 7 rows of Garter st. Break MC, leaving sts on needle.

Take the second row of squares (Squares 3-6-5-4) and with RS facing, MC, and second smaller circular needles, PU and K 64 sts from first CO edge (Square 3), *PU and K 8 sts across Garter st edge, PU and K 64 sts from next CO edge; rep from * to end. 280 sts.
Work 7 rows of Garter st as before, but do not break yarn.
Turn as if to work another row (RS facing) and place bottom row of squares in front of it with WS facing you. Using yarn from needle behind, join using a 3-Needle Bind Off.

Rep to join next four rows.

Outer Edging

Top and Bottom Edges
With RS facing, using MC and smaller circular needles, PU and K 280 sts across top of throw as before.
Work 16 rows of Garter st, ending with a RS row.
BO K-wise on WS.

Rep for bottom of throw.

Side Edges
With RS facing, at top side edge using MC and smaller circular needles, PU and K 9 sts from Garter st edge, PU and K 63 sts from LH side of first square, *PU and K 8 sts from Garter st edge, PU and K 63 sts from LH side of next square; rep from * four more times, PU and K 9 sts from bottom Garter st edge. 436 sts.
Work 16 rows of Garter st, ending with a RS row.
BO K-wise on WS.

Rep for RH side of throw, beginning at lower RS edge.

Finishing

Weave in ends. As all squares have already been individually blocked prior to joining, it is not essential to wash and block entire throw to diagram, but you may wish to.

1	4	3	2
4	5	6	3
1	6	5	2
2	5	6	1
3	6	5	4
2	3	4	1

A 55.5"
B 79.5"
C 12.75"
D 12.5"

Nevern Chart 1

LEGEND

■ Main Color

□ Contrasting Color

□ K
RS: Knit stitch
WS: Purl stitch

Nevern Chart 3

Nevern Chart 5

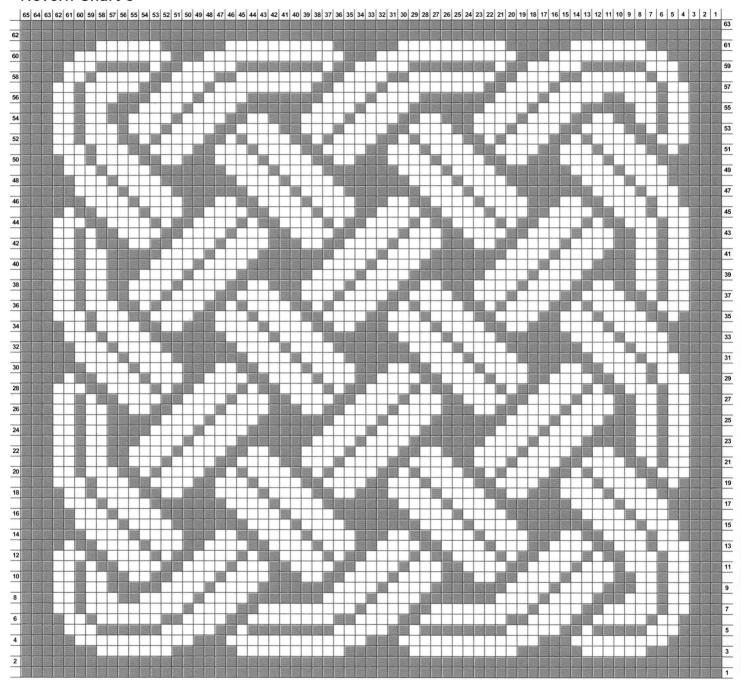

Nevern Chart 2

Nevern Chart 4

Nevern Chart 6

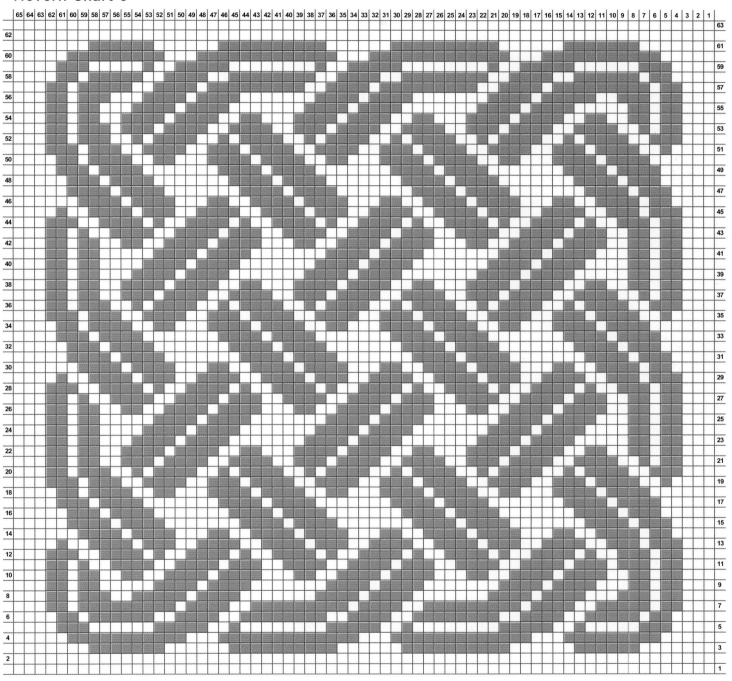

Nevern Throw 79

NUALLAN CAPE & CAPELET

by Jen Pierce

FINISHED MEASUREMENTS
54 (62, 70)" full body circumference at bustline, to fit sizes S/M (L/XL, 2X/3X) (measured 11 (11, 12)" from top of shoulder); meant to be worn with plenty of ease
Capelet 16 (17.5, 19)" body length from top of shoulder
Cape 27 (30, 33)" body length from top of shoulder
Sample is S/M Cape; model is 34" bust

YARN
Wool of the Andes™ (worsted weight, 100% Peruvian Highland Wool; 110 yards/50g): Forest Heather 23897
Capelet 12 (14, 16) skeins
Cape 16 (19, 21) skeins

NEEDLES
US 4 (3.5mm) 16" circular needles, or size to obtain gauge
US 6 (4mm) 16" and 32" circular needles, or size to obtain gauge

NOTIONS
Yarn Needle
Stitch Markers
Cable Needle
Scrap Yarn or Stitch Holders

GAUGE
20 sts and 31 rows = 4" in Basket Weave on larger needles, blocked
32 sts and 28 rows = 4" in Plait Cable on larger needles, blocked
16 sts and 48 rows = 4" in Fisherman's Rib on smaller needles, blocked

For pattern support, contact indigohillknits@gmail.com

Nuallan Cape & Capelet

Notes:
This elegant Celtic-inspired cape features a dramatic cabled front panel, Basket Weave detail, unique braid cable edge finish, and a cozy fisherman's rib collar. Nuallan is a show-stopping throw-on layer perfect for chilly days or nights.

The Nuallan cape can be made in two lengths: a shorter capelet reaching the elbow, or a mid-length cape ending at the hips. Both lengths are worked in the round from the top down to the elbow; the mid-length cape is then split into front and back panels, which are worked flat. Braid cable edging is knit separately and seamed to the cape.

Charts are worked both in the round and flat. When working charts in the round, read each chart row from right to left as a RS row; when working charts flat, read RS rows (odd numbers) from right to left, and WS rows (even numbers) from left to right. Horseshoe cable chart and Plait cable chart are worked both flat and in the round—be sure to use RS st instructions for working in the round.

M1R-P (make 1 right-leaning purl stitch)
Inserting LH needle from back to front, PU horizontal strand between st just worked and next st, and P into it.

M1L-P (make 1 left-leaning purl stitch)
Inserting LH needle from front to back, PU horizontal strand between st just worked and next st, and P into the back loop.

Fisherman's Rib (in the round over an even number of sts)
Rnd 1: (K into the st below, P1) to end of rnd.
Rnd 2: (K1, P into the st below) to end of rnd.
Rep Rnds 1-2 for pattern.

Basket Weave (in the round over a multiple of 8 sts plus 5)
Rnd 1: K all.
Rnds 2-4: P1, (P4, K3, P1) to last 4 sts, P4.
Rnd 5: K all.
Rnds 6-8: P1, (K3, P5) to last 4 sts, K3, P1.
Rep Rnds 1-8 for pattern.

Basket Weave (flat over a multiple of 8 sts plus 5)
Row 1 (RS): K across.
Row 2 (WS): K4, (K1, P3, K4) to last st, K1.
Row 3: P1, (P4, K3, P1) to last 4 sts, P4.
Row 4: Rep Row 2.
Row 5: K across.
Row 6: K1, P3, (K5, P3) to last st, K1.
Row 7: P1, (K3, P5) to last 4 sts, K3, P1.
Row 8: Rep Row 6.
Rep Rows 1-8 for pattern.

See here for a tutorial for the optional Long Tail Tubular Cast On method: blog.knitpicks.com/long-tail-tubular-cast-on

Vertical to Horizontal Mattress Stitch
Work vertically across columns of selvedge of border piece, using yarn needle to PU bars between sts, and horizontally across bottom edge, picking up under the point of the Vs. Since there are more rows than sts to the inch, it is necessary to pick up more vertical bars than horizontal Vs, to prevent the edge from puckering. Try picking up two bars for every third V; it may be necessary to experiment a bit to get a neat edge, using pinned fabric as a guide.

DIRECTIONS

Collar
Using smaller 16" circular needles, CO 96 (112, 112) sts using Long Tail Tubular Cast On method for 1x1 Rib, starting with a K st; do not join. Or, use CO of choice—if using a different CO, skip the following foundation rows.

Foundation Row 1: (K1 TBL, Sl1 WYIF) to end.
Foundation Row 2: (K1, Sl1 WYIF) to end.

Join to work in the rnd, being careful not to twist sts; PM for BOR.
Setup Rnd: (K1, P1) to end.
Work Fisherman's Rib until collar measures 10 (12, 12)", or desired length.

Neck
Switch to larger size 16" circular needles.

Sizes 62" & 70" Only
(K7, M1) to end of rnd. 16 sts inc, 128 sts.

Size 70" Only
(K4, M1) to end of rnd. 32 sts inc, 160 sts.

Resume All Sizes
Setup Rnd: K5 (13, 21) for right sleeve, PM, K41 (49, 57) for front, PM, K5 (13, 21) for left sleeve, PM, K45 (53, 61) for back to BOR M.

Short Row 1 (RS): K1, M1L, K to 1 st before M, M1R, K1, SM, KFB, W&T. 2 sts inc on right sleeve, 1 st inc on right front.
Short Row 2 (WS): P2, SM, P right sleeve to M, SM, PFB, K4, P3, (K5, P3) to 5 sts before M, K4, PFB, SM, P1, M1L-P, P3, M1R-P, P1, SM, PFB, W&T. 2 sts inc on back, 2 sts inc on left sleeve, 1 st inc on left front.
Short Row 3 (RS): K2, SM, K left sleeve to M, SM, K1, P5, (K3, P5) to 1 st before M, K1, SM, K1, M1L, K to 1 st before M, M1R, K1, SM, K1, KFB, K next st tog with wrap, W&T. 2 sts inc on right sleeve, 1 st inc on right front.
Short Row 4 (WS): P to M, SM, P right sleeve to M, SM, PFB, (K5, P3) to 6 sts before M, K5, PFB, SM, P1, M1L-P, P left sleeve to 1 st before M, M1R-P, P1, SM, P1, PFB, P next st tog with wrap, W&T. 2 sts inc on back, 2 sts inc on left sleeve, 1 st inc on left front.

Short Row 5 (RS): K to M, SM, K left sleeve to M, SM, K back to M, SM, K1, M1L, K to 1 st before M, M1R, K1, SM, K1, KFB, K1, W&T. 2 sts inc on right sleeve, 1 st inc on right front.

Short Row 6 (WS): P to M, SM, P right sleeve to M, SM, PFB, K2, P3, (K5, P3) to 3 sts before M, K2, PFB, SM, P1, M1L-P, P left sleeve to 1 st before M, M1R-P, P1, SM, P1, PFB, P1, W&T. 2 sts inc on back, 2 sts inc on left sleeve, 1 st inc on left front.

Short Row 7 (RS): K to M, SM, K left sleeve to M, SM, K1, P3, K3, (P5, K3) to 4 sts before M, P3, K1, SM, K1, M1L, K to 1 st before M, M1R, K1, SM, K1, KFB, K1, W&T. 2 sts inc on right sleeve, 1 st inc on right front.

Short Row 8 (WS): P to M, SM, P right sleeve to M, SM, PFB, K3, P3, (K5, P3) to 4 sts before M, K3, PFB, SM, P1, M1L-P, P left sleeve to 1 st before M, M1R-P, P1, SM, P1, PFB, P1, W&T. 2 sts inc on back, 2 sts inc on left sleeve, 1 st inc on left front.

Short Row 9 (RS): K to M, SM, K left sleeve to M, SM, K back to M, SM.

128 (160, 192) sts; 49 (57, 65) front sts, 53 (61, 69) back sts, 13 (21, 29) sts per sleeve (8 sts inc per section, 32 sts inc total).

Shoulders

Resume working in the rnd. Switch to longer circular needles when needed.

Setup Rnd 1: Working wraps tog with sts when reached, *K1, (K3, P5) to 4 sts before M, K4, SM* (right sleeve), K1, P1, K6, P1, P0 (4, 8), K31, P0 (4, 8), P1, K6, P1, K1, SM (front); rep from * to * two more times (left sleeve, back).

Setup Rnd 2 (Inc): *K1, M1L, (K3, P5) to 4 sts before M, K3, M1R, K1, SM* (right sleeve), K1, M1L, P1, K6, P1, P0 (4, 8), PM for edge of Plait Cable, (K1, KFB) 14 times, K3, PM for edge of Plait Cable, P0 (4, 8), P1, K6, P1, M1R, K1, SM (front); rep from * to * two more times (left sleeve, back). 14 sts inc for front cable; 45 sts between front Plait Cable Ms. 22 total sts inc; 150 (182, 214) sts.

Setup Rnd 3: *K2, (K3, P5) to 5 sts before M, K5, SM* (right sleeve), K2, P1, K6, P1, P0 (4, 8), SM, K3, (P4, K6) four times, P2, SM, P0 (4, 8), P1, K6, P1, K2, SM (front); rep from * to * two more times (left sleeve, back).

Upper Body

Cont working Basket Weave as established on sleeves and back using Shoulder Back chart; work pattern rep 1 (2, 3) times for sleeves, and 6 (7, 8) times for back.

Rnd 1 (Inc): Work Shoulder Back chart for right sleeve, SM, work Shoulder Right Front chart, PM for body inc, M1L, P0 (4, 8), SM, work Plait Cable chart, SM, P0 (4, 8), M1R, PM for body inc, work Shoulder Left Front chart, SM, work Shoulder Back chart for left sleeve, SM, work Shoulder Back chart for back.

Rnd 2: Work Shoulder Back for right sleeve, SM, work Shoulder Right Front, SM, P to M, SM, work Plait Cable, SM, P to M, SM, work Shoulder Left Front, SM, work Shoulder Back for left sleeve, SM, work Shoulder Back for back.

Rnds 3-8: Rep Rnd 2.

Rnd 9 (Front Body Inc): Work Shoulder Back for right sleeve, SM, work Shoulder Right Front, SM, M1L-P, P to M, SM, work Plait Cable, SM, P to M, M1R-P, SM, work Shoulder Left Front, SM, work Shoulder Back for left sleeve, SM, work Shoulder Back for back.

Rnds 10-16: Rep Rnd 2.

218 (250, 282) sts; 85 (93, 101) front sts, 71 (79, 87) back sts, 31 (39, 47) sts per sleeve.

Extend the Basket Weave pattern to both edges of all Basket Weave sections, incorporating incs, being careful to keep pattern aligned. Note that on Rnd 17, working Basket Weave as established means working Rnd 1 of Basket Weave pattern (K all Basket Weave sts).

(Pattern continues after charts.)

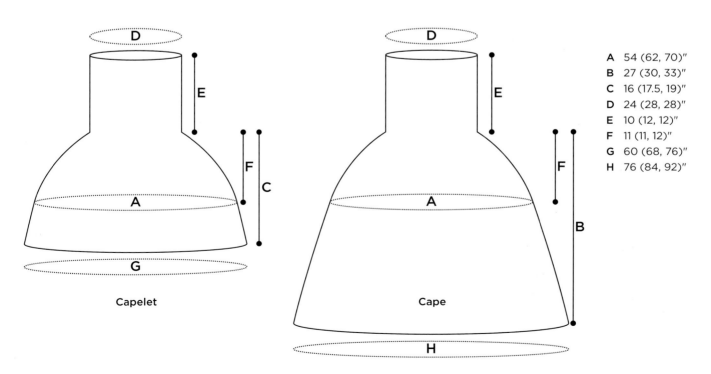

Capelet

Cape

A 54 (62, 70)"
B 27 (30, 33)"
C 16 (17.5, 19)"
D 24 (28, 28)"
E 10 (12, 12)"
F 11 (11, 12)"
G 60 (68, 76)"
H 76 (84, 92)"

Shoulder Back

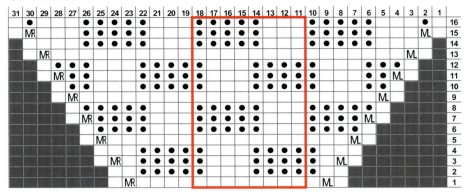

Plait Cable

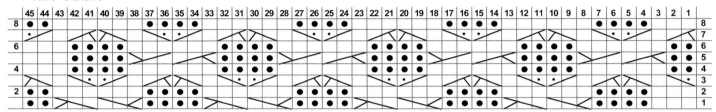

LEGEND

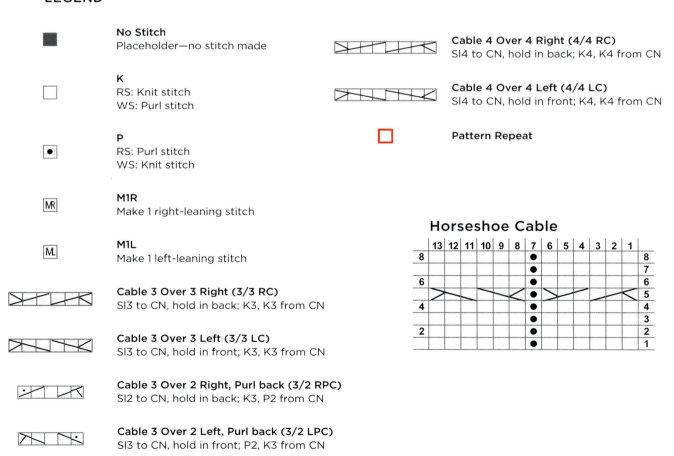

Horseshoe Cable

Shoulder Left Front

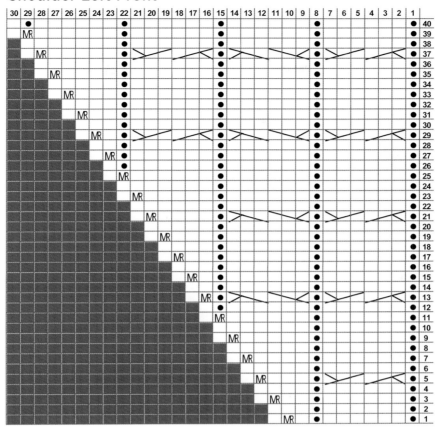

Shoulder Right Front

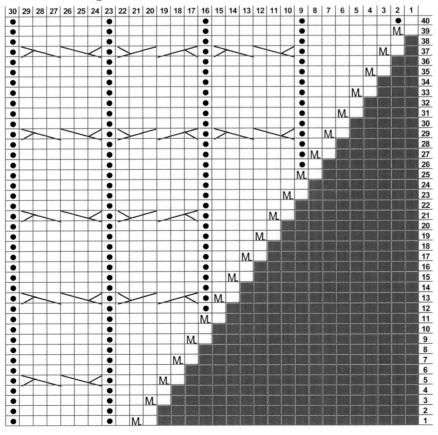

Rnd 17 (Inc): *K1, M1L, work Basket Weave as established to 1 st before M, M1R, K1, SM*, work Shoulder Right Front, SM, M1L-P, P to M, SM, work Plait Cable, SM, P to M, M1R-P, SM, work Shoulder Left Front, SM; rep from * to * two more times.

Rnds 18-24: *K1, work Basket Weave as established to 1 st before M, extending pattern to include inc sts at each edge, K1, SM*, work Shoulder Right Front, SM, P to M, SM, work Plait Cable, SM, P to M, SM, work Shoulder Left Front, SM; rep from * to * two more times.

Rep Rnds 17-24 two more times.

Shoulder Left Front and Shoulder Right Front charts are completed. Last rnd worked should be Row 8 of Plait Cable chart and Basket Weave pattern.

266 (298, 330) sts on needles: 115 (123, 131) front sts, 77 (85, 93) back sts, 37 (45, 53) sts per sleeve.

Middle Body

Rnd 1 (Inc): *K1, M1L, work Basket Weave as established to 1 st before M, M1R, K1, SM*, K1, P1, (work Horseshoe Cable chart, P1) two times, SM, M1L-P, P to M, SM, work Plait Cable, SM, P to M, M1R-P, SM, P1, (work Horseshoe Cable chart, P1) two times, K1, SM; rep from * to * two more times. 8 sts inc.

Rnds 2-8: *K1, work Basket Weave as established to 1 st before M, extending pattern to edges, K1, SM*, K1, P1, (work Horseshoe Cable, P1) two times, SM, P to M, SM, work Plait Cable, SM, P to M, SM, P1, (work Horseshoe Cable, P1) two times, K1, SM; rep from * to * two more times.

For Capelet length: Rep Rnds 1-8 until work measures approx 14 (15.5, 17)" from top of shoulder, or 2" shorter than desired length, ending with Rnd 8. Discontinue incs and WE once 338 (370, 418) sts are reached. Cont to Border Braid section.

For Cape length: Rep Rnds 1-8 until work measures approx 16 (18, 20)" from top of shoulder, ending with Rnd 8. Cont to Split for Arm Slits.

Split for Arm Slits

To create arm slits, separate front and back panels at this point and work the rest of each panel flat. The slits will be placed between the columns of inverted horseshoe cables.

Setup Rnd: Sl sts onto scrap yarn or st holder up to first M, SM, Sl 16 more sts onto holder—this is part of the back panel; using a new piece of scrap yarn or st holder, Sl 14 sts to holder, SM, Sl P sts to next M, SM, Sl 45 Plait Cable sts, SM, Sl P sts to next M, SM, Sl 14 sts—this is the entire front panel.

Next Rnd: Sl held back panel sts onto working needle. The front panel is now set aside, and all back panel sts are on the needles.

Back Panel

Work back panel flat from this point. Do not turn work yet; instead, break previous yarn and join new yarn, ready to work RS.

Work charts flat as established, starting with Row 1.
At beginning and end of the first Row 1, BO one edge st per side as instructed; do not work BOs on following Row 1 reps.

Row 1 (RS, Inc): BO 1 st (starting row only), work Horseshoe Cable, P1, K1, SM, (K1, M1L, work Basket Weave (flat) to 1 st before M, M1R, K1, SM) three times, K1, P1, work Horseshoe Cable, BO 1 at end (starting row only), turn work. 6 sts inc; 2 sts BO on starting row only.

Rows 2, 4, 6, 8 (WS): Work Horseshoe Cable, K1, P1, SM, (P1, work Basket Weave (flat) to 1 st before M, P1, SM) three times, P1, K1, work Horseshoe Cable, turn work.

Rows 3, 5, 7 (RS): Work Horseshoe Cable, P1, K1, SM, (K1, work Basket Weave (flat) to 1 st before M, K1, SM) three times, K1, P1, work Horseshoe Cable, turn work.

Rep Rows 1-8, omitting BOs on subsequent Inc rows, until work measures approx 25 (28, 31)" from top of shoulder, or 2" shorter than desired length.
BO these sts.

Front Panel

Sl all front panel sts from holder onto needles, ready to work RS.

Row 1 (RS, Inc): Work Horseshoe Cable, P1, SM, M1L-P, P to M, SM, work Plait Cable, SM, P to M, M1R-P, SM, P1, work Horseshoe Cable, turn work. 2 sts inc.

Rows 2, 4, 6, 8 (WS): Work Horseshoe Cable, K1, SM, K to M, SM, work Plait Cable, SM, K to M, SM, K1, work Horseshoe Cable, turn work.

Rows 3, 5, 7 (RS): Work Horseshoe Cable, P1, SM, P to M, SM, work Plait Cable, SM, P to M, SM, P1, work Horseshoe Cable, turn work.

Rep Rows 1-8 until work measures approx 25 (28, 31)" from top of shoulder, or 2" shorter than desired length, matching length of finished back panel.
BO these sts.

Border Braid

Before beginning border braid, wash and block finished piece to diagram.

For Capelet length: Measure bottom circumference. Knit border braid in one piece until length of braid equals bottom circumference.

For Cape length: Measure bottom edges of front and back panels. Knit two border braids, one matching front panel edge length and one matching back panel edge length.

Work Border Braid chart until braid measures desired length(s).

Wash and block border braid. It may be helpful to block before binding off, in order to make adjustments. Loosely pin braid to blocked piece. Add or remove a few rows of border braid if needed to match edge lengths, then BO.

Finishing

After all the pieces have been washed and blocked, and loosely pinned together, seam border braid to garment bottom edge, using Vertical to Horizontal Mattress Stitch.

Weave in ends. At top collar edge, if using a Tubular Cast On, use tail from CO to seam small gap left by foundation rows before weaving in.

Border Braid

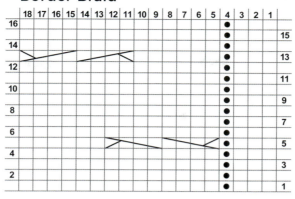

PARTING OF THE WAYS PULLOVER

by Theresa Shingler

FINISHED MEASUREMENTS
33 (35.75, 38.25, 41, 43.75, 46.25, 49, 51.75, 54.25, 57, 59.75, 62.25)" finished bust circumference; meant to be worn with 4-6" positive ease
Sample is 38.25" size; model is 34" bust

YARN
Simply Wool™ (worsted weight, 100% Eco Wool; 218 yards/100g): Wanda 27468, 5 (6, 6, 7, 7, 8, 8, 8, 9, 9, 10, 10) hanks

NEEDLES
US 8 (5mm) DPNs, and 32-48" circular needles, or size to obtain gauge

NOTIONS
Yarn Needle
10 Stitch Markers (named M-1 through M-6 and M-A through M-D)
Cable Needle
Scrap Yarn or Stitch Holders

GAUGE
33 sts and 26 rnds = 4" in Center Cable Chart in the round, blocked
18 sts and 26 rows = 4" in Stockinette Stitch in the round and flat, blocked

For pattern support, contact theresashinglerknits@gmail.com

Parting of the Ways Pullover

Notes:

Inspired by the flowing, maze-like braids in illuminated Celtic medieval manuscripts, the striking central cable panel on this sweater moves up the front and back of the body, splits into separate braids to encompass the neck, and then joins at the shoulders.

Parting of the Ways is worked in the round from the hem up. The central cable panel splits with increases that make space for the neckline and create an exaggerated drop shoulder silhouette. The front and back separate at the underarm, arms are picked up and worked in the round from armhole to cuff, and the neckline is picked up and worked in the round.

Charts are worked both in the round and flat. In the round, read each chart row from right to left as a RS row; flat, read RS rows (odd numbers) from right to left, and WS rows (even numbers) from left to right.

LT (left twist)
Sl1 to CN, hold in front; K1, K1 from CN.

RT (right twist)
Sl1 to CN, hold in back; K1, K1 from CN.

3/3 LC (3 over 3 left cable)
Sl3 to CN, hold in front; K3, K3 from CN.

3/3 RC (3 over 3 right cable)
Sl3 to CN, hold in back; K3, K3 from CN.

3/3 LPC (3 over 3 left cable, purl back)
Sl3 to CN, hold in front; P3, K3 from CN.

3/3 RPC (3 over 3 right cable, purl back)
Sl3 to CN, hold in back; K3, P3 from CN.

Center Cable chart (in the round over 48 sts)
Rnd 1: P1, RT, LT, P1, K3, (P6, 3/3 RC) two times, P6, K3, P1, RT, LT, P1.
Rnd 2: P1, K4, P1, K3, (P6, K6) two times, P6, K3, P1, K4, P1.
Rnd 3: P1, RT, LT, P1, (3/3 LPC, 3/3 RPC) three times, P1, RT, LT, P1.
Rnd 4: P1, K4, P4, (K6, P6) two times, K6, P4, K4, P1.
Rnd 5: P1, RT, LT, P4, (3/3 LC, P6) two times, 3/3 LC, P4, RT, LT, P1.
Rnd 6: Rep Rnd 4.
Rnd 7: P1, RT, LT, P1, (3/3 RPC, 3/3 LPC) three times, P1, RT, LT, P1.
Rnd 8: Rep Rnd 2.
Rep Rnds 1-8 for pattern.

Split Cable Left chart (in the round over 24 sts)
Rnd 1: P1, RT, LT, P1, K3, P6, 3/3 RC, P3.
Rnd 2: P1, K4, P1, K3, P6, K6, P3.
Rnd 3: P1, RT, LT, P1, 3/3 LPC, 3/3 LPC, 3/3 RPC.
Rnd 4: P1, K4, P4, K6, P6, K3.
Rnd 5: P1, RT, LT, P4, 3/3 LC, P6, K3.
Rnd 6: Rep Rnd 4.
Rnd 7: P1, RT, LT, P1, 3/3 RPC, 3/3 LPC, 3/3 RPC.
Rnd 8: Rep Rnd 2.
Rep Rnds 1-8 for pattern.

Split Cable Left chart (flat over 24 sts)
Row 1 (RS): P1, RT, LT, P1, K3, P6, 3/3 RC, P3.
Row 2 (WS): K3, P6, K6, P3, K1, P4, K1.
Row 3: P1, RT, LT, P1, 3/3 LPC, 3/3 RPC, 3/3 LPC.
Row 4: P3, K6, P6, K4, P4, K1.
Row 5: P1, RT, LT, P4, 3/3 LC, P6, K3.
Row 6: Rep Row 4.
Row 7: P1, RT, LT, P1, 3/3 RPC, 3/3 LPC, 3/3 RPC.
Row 8: Rep Row 2.
Rep Rows 1-8 for pattern.

Split Cable Right chart (in the round over 24 sts)
Rnd 1: P3, 3/3 RC, P6, K3, P1, RT, LT, P1.
Rnd 2: P3, K6, P6, K3, P1, K4, P1.
Rnd 3: 3/3 RPC, 3/3 LPC, 3/3 RPC, P1, RT, LT, P1.
Rnd 4: K3, P6, K6, P4, K4, P1.
Rnd 5: K3, P6, 3/3 RC, P4, RT, LT, P1.
Rnd 6: Rep Rnd 4.
Rnd 7: 3/3 LPC, 3/3 RPC, 3/3 LPC, P1, RT, LT, P1.
Rnd 8: Rep Rnd 2.
Rep Rnds 1-8 for pattern.

Split Cable Right chart (flat over 24 sts)
Row 1 (RS): P3, 3/3 RC, P6, K3, P1, RT, LT, P1.
Row 2 (WS): K1, P4, K1, P3, K6, P6, K3.
Row 3: 3/3 RPC, 3/3 LPC, 3/3 RPC, P1, RT, LT, P1.
Row 4: K1, P4, K4, P6, K6, P3.
Row 5: K3, P6, 3/3 RC, P4, RT, LT, P1.
Row 6: Rep Row 4.
Row 7: 3/3 LPC, 3/3 RPC, 3/3 LPC, P1, RT, LT, P1.
Row 8: Rep Row 2.
Rep Rows 1–8 for pattern.

DIRECTIONS

Body

Using preferred method, loosely CO 192 (204, 216, 228, 240, 252, 264, 276, 288, 300, 312, 324) sts. Join for working in the rnd, being careful not to twist sts, PM for BOR.
Rnds 1-12: (K3, P3) to end. Remove M at end of final rnd.

Setup Rnd: K0 (5, 0, 5, 0, 5, 0, 5, 0, 5, 0, 5) PM-1 for BOR, P24 (27, 30, 33, 36, 39, 42, 45, 48, 51, 54, 57), PM-2, work Rnd 1 of Center Cable chart, PM-3, P24 (27, 30, 33, 36, 39, 42, 45, 48, 51, 54, 57), PM-4, P24 (27, 30, 33, 36, 39, 42, 45, 48, 51, 54, 57), PM-5, work Rnd 1 of Center Cable chart, PM-6, P24 (27, 30, 33, 36, 39, 42, 45, 48, 51, 54, 57).

Cont as established, working Center Cable between Ms 2 & 3 and Ms 5 & 6, until work measures 17.5 (17.5, 18.75, 18.75, 18.75, 18.75, 18.75, 17.5, 17.5, 18.75, 18.75, 18.75)" from CO edge, ending on Rnd 7 of Center Cable chart.

Cable Split Increases

Setup Rnd: Work as established to M-2, work Sts 1-21 of Center Cable, P1, PFB, PM-A, P2, PM-B, P1, PFB, work Sts 28-48 of Center Cable, work as established to M-5, work Sts 1-21 of Center Cable, P1, PFB, PM-C, P2, PM-D, P1, PFB, work Sts 28-48 of Center Cable, work as established to end. 196 (208, 220, 232, 244, 256, 268, 280, 292, 304, 316, 328) sts.

Rnd 1: Work as established to M-2, work Split Cable Left chart to M-A, P2, SM, work Split Cable Right chart to M-3, work as established to M-5, work Split Cable Left to M-C, P2, SM, work to Split Cable Right, SM, work as established to end.

Rnd 2: Work as established to M-A, (PFB) twice, SM, work as established to M-C, (PFB) twice, work as established to end. 200 (212, 224, 236, 248, 260, 272, 284, 296, 308 320, 332) sts.

Rnd 3: Work as established to M-A, P to M-B, work as established to M-C, P to M-D, work as established to end.

Rnd 4: Work as established to M-A, PFB, P to 1 st before M-B, PFB, SM, work as established to M-C, PFB, P to 1 st before M-D, PFB, SM, work to end. 4 sts inc.

Rnd 5: Rep Rnd 3.

Rep Rnds 4-5 until work measures 18.5 (18.25, 19.5, 19.5, 19.5, 19.75, 19.5, 18.5, 18.75, 19.75, 19.5, 19.5)" from CO edge.

Front

Row 1 (RS): Work even as established to M-4. Turn work to begin working flat.

Row 2 (WS): K to M-3, work Split Cable Right (flat) to M-B, KFB, K to 1 st before M-A, KFB, SM, work Split Cable Left (flat) to M-2, K to end.

Rep Rows 1-2 until there are 30 (32, 34, 38, 38, 40, 40, 40, 42, 42, 42, 44) sts between Ms A & B. 126 (134, 142, 152, 158, 166, 172, 178, 186, 192, 198, 206) Front sts.

Front Neck Shaping

Work as established to M-A, P10 (11, 12, 13, 13, 14, 14, 14, 14, 14, 14, 15), BO 10 (10, 10, 12, 12, 12, 12, 12, 14, 14, 14, 14), P10 (11, 12, 13, 13, 14, 14, 14, 14, 14, 14, 15), SM, work as established to end. 58 (62, 66, 70, 73, 77, 80, 83, 86, 89, 92, 96) sts each shoulder.

Right Shoulder

Row 1 (WS): Work as established to end.
Row 2 (RS): P2tog, work as established to end. 1 st dec.
Rep Rows 1-2 8 (9, 10, 11, 11, 12, 12, 12, 12, 12, 12, 13) more times.
49 (52, 55, 58, 61, 64, 67, 70, 73, 76, 79, 82) sts.
Place sts on st holder or scrap yarn.

Left Shoulder

Join yarn at neck edge ready to begin a WS row.
Row 1 (WS): K2tog, work as established to end. 1 st dec.
Row 2 (RS): Work as established to end.
Rep Rows 1-2 8 (9, 10, 11, 11, 12, 12, 12, 12, 12, 12, 13) more times.
49 (52, 55, 58, 61, 64, 67, 70, 73, 76, 79, 82) sts.
Place sts on st holder or scrap yarn.

Back

Work as for Front until Front Neck Shaping. 26 (134, 142, 152, 158, 166, 172, 178, 186, 192, 198, 206) Back sts.

Row 1: Work as established to M-C, P to M-D, SM, work as established to end.
Row 2: Work as established to M-D, K to M-C, SM, work as established to end.
Rep Rows 1-2 6 (6, 5, 6, 6, 6, 6, 8, 7, 7, 7, 7) more times.

(Pattern continues after charts.)

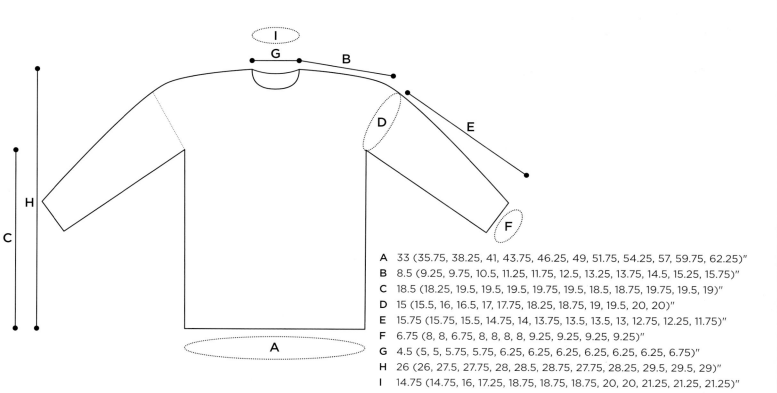

- **A** 33 (35.75, 38.25, 41, 43.75, 46.25, 49, 51.75, 54.25, 57, 59.75, 62.25)"
- **B** 8.5 (9.25, 9.75, 10.5, 11.25, 11.75, 12.5, 13.25, 13.75, 14.5, 15.25, 15.75)"
- **C** 18.5 (18.25, 19.5, 19.5, 19.5, 19.75, 19.5, 18.5, 18.75, 19.75, 19.5, 19)"
- **D** 15 (15.5, 16, 16.5, 17, 17.75, 18.25, 18.75, 19, 19.5, 20, 20)"
- **E** 15.75 (15.75, 15.5, 14.75, 14, 13.75, 13.5, 13.5, 13, 12.75, 12.25, 11.75)"
- **F** 6.75 (8, 8, 6.75, 8, 8, 8, 8, 9.25, 9.25, 9.25, 9.25)"
- **G** 4.5 (5, 5, 5.75, 5.75, 6.25, 6.25, 6.25, 6.25, 6.25, 6.25, 6.75)"
- **H** 26 (26, 27.5, 27.75, 28, 28.5, 28.75, 27.75, 28.25, 29.5, 29.5, 29)"
- **I** 14.75 (14.75, 16, 17.25, 18.75, 18.75, 18.75, 20, 20, 21.25, 21.25, 21.25)"

LEGEND

- ☐ Knit Stitch
- ⊡ Purl Stitch
- Right Twist (RT): Sl1 to CN, hold in back; K1, K1 from CN
- Left Twist (LT): Sl1 to CN, hold in front; K1, K1 from CN
- Cable 3 Over 3 Right (3/3 RC): Sl3 to CN, hold in back; K3, K3 from CN
- Cable 3 Over 3 Left (3/3 LC): Sl3 to CN, hold in front; K3, K3 from CN
- Cable 3 Over 3 Right, Purl back (3/3 RPC): Sl3 to CN, hold in back; K3, P3 from CN
- Cable 3 Over 3 Left, Purl back (3/3 LPC): Sl3 to CN, hold in front; P3, K3 from CN

Center Cable

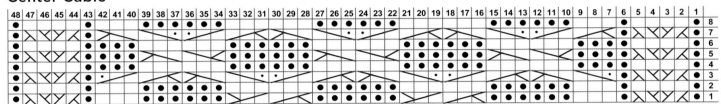

Split Cable Left

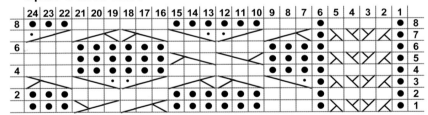

Split Cable Right

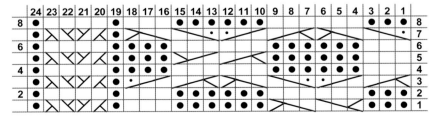

Back Neckline Shaping
Work as established to M-C, P5 (5, 6, 6, 6, 6, 6, 6, 7, 7, 7, 7), BO 20 (22, 22, 26, 26, 28, 28, 28, 28, 28, 28, 30), P5 (5, 6, 6, 6, 6, 6, 6, 7, 7, 7, 7) SM, work as established to end. 53 (56, 60, 63, 66, 69, 72, 75, 79, 82, 85, 88) sts each shoulder.

Left Shoulder
Row 1 (WS): Work as established to end.
Row 2 (PS): P2tog, work as established to end. 1 st dec.
Rep Rows 1-2 3 (3, 4, 4, 4, 4, 4, 4, 5, 5, 5, 5) more times. 49 (52, 55, 58, 61, 64, 67, 70, 73, 76, 79, 82) sts.
Place sts on st holder or scrap yarn.

Right Shoulder
Join yarn at neck edge ready to begin a WS row.
Row 1 (WS): K2tog, work as established to end. 1 st dec.
Row 2 (RS): Work as established to end.
Rep Rows 1-2 3 (3, 4, 4, 4, 4, 4, 4, 5, 5, 5, 5) more times. 49 (52, 55, 58, 61, 64, 67, 70, 73, 76, 79, 82) sts.

With WS facing use 3-Needle Bind Off to join Front and Back shoulder seams tog.

Sleeves (make two the same)
Beginning at bottom middle of underarm, PU and P 68 (70, 72, 74, 76, 80, 82, 84, 86, 88, 90, 90) sts. PM for BOR.
Rnd 1: P all.
Rep Rnd 1 6 (16, 9, 19, 11, 0, 18, 14, 17, 13, 6, 3) more times.

Dec Rnd: P2tog, P to 2 sts before M, P2tog TBL. 2 sts dec.
Rep Dec Rnd every 4 (4, 4, 3, 3, 3, 3, 3, 3, 3, 3) rnds, 18 (16, 17, 18, 19, 21, 22, 23, 21, 22, 23, 23) more times. 30 (36, 36, 36, 36, 36, 36, 36, 42, 42, 42, 42) sts.
WE until Sleeve measures approx 2" shorter than desired length (if necessary).

Cuff
Rnds 1-8: (K3, P3) to end.
BO sts.

Neckline
Beginning at back neck, PU and K 20 (22, 22, 26, 26, 28, 28, 28, 28, 28, 28, 30) sts along back neck BO, PU and K 18 (17, 20, 20, 23, 22, 22, 25, 24, 27, 27, 27) sts down side of neck decs, PU and K 10 (10, 10, 12, 12, 12, 12, 12, 14, 14, 14, 14) sts along front neck BO, PU and K 18 (17, 20, 20, 23, 22, 22, 25, 24, 27, 27, 27) sts up side of neck decs. PM for BOR. 66 (66, 72, 78, 84, 84, 84, 90, 90, 96, 96, 96) sts.

Rnds 1-8: (K3, P3) to end.
BO sts.

Finishing
Weave in ends, wash, and block to diagram.

SENNIT VEST

by Margaret Mills

FINISHED MEASUREMENTS
33.75 (37.25, 41, 44.5, 48.25, 51.75, 56.5, 60.25, 63.75)" finished bust circumference; meant to be worn with 2-6" positive ease
Sample is 37.25" size; model is 34" bust

YARN
Simply Wool™ (worsted weight, 100% Eco Wool; 218 yards/100g): Wilhelmina 27471, 5 (5, 6, 7, 7, 7, 9, 10, 11) hanks

NEEDLES
US 7 (4.5mm) DPNs, and straight or circular needles, or size to obtain gauge

NOTIONS
Yarn Needle
Stitch Markers
Cable Needle
Scrap Yarn or Stitch Holder

GAUGE
22 sts and 30 rows = 4" in Moss Stitch, blocked
36 sts = 4.75" over sts 3-38 of Diamond Chart, blocked (sts 3-10 = 1.0625"; sts 11-28 = 3.6875")
30 rows = 4" in Diamond Chart, blocked

For pattern support, contact margaretgracemills@gmail.com

Sennit Vest

Notes:

Fishermen used fancy knotwork to cover a ship's wheels and rails for easier gripping in wet conditions, and the work kept them entertained on long voyages. Sennit's cables echo this fancywork, with the lines crossing between the main and edging cables and even the cabled ribbing.

The Sennit Vest is worked flat in two pieces from the bottom up. The 36 stitch wide and 36 row long cable chart is repeated several times across the width of both front and back. Cable ribbing is worked in the round on both neck and armholes after seaming.

Some charts are worked flat and some are worked in the round. For Cable Rib—Flat and Diamond Cable, read RS rows (odd numbers) from right to left, and WS rows (even numbers) from left to right. For Collar Transition and Cable Rib—Round, read each chart row from right to left as a RS row.

2/1 LIC (cable 2 over 1 left, increase back)
Sl2 to CN, hold in front; KFB, K2 from CN. 1 st inc.

2/2 LDC (cable 2 over 2 left, decrease back)
Sl2 to CN, hold in front; K2tog, K2 from CN. 1 st dec.

Cable Rib—Flat (flat over a multiple of 6 sts plus 2, after setup)
On RS rows, Sl first st P-wise WYIB; on WS rows, Sl first st P-wise WYIF.
Setup Row 1 (RS): Sl1, (P1, K3, P1) to last st, K1.
Setup Row 2 (WS): Sl1, (K1, P3, K1) to last st, P1.
Setup Row 3: Sl1, (P1, 2/2 LIC, P1) to last st, K1. 1 st inc per rep.
Row 4 (WS): Sl1, (K1, P4, K1) to last st, P1.
Row 5 (RS): Sl1, (P1, K4, P1) to last st, K1.
Row 6: Rep Row 3.
Row 7: Sl1, (P1, 2/2 LC, P1) to last st, K1.
Rep Rows 4-7 for pattern.

Moss Stitch (flat over any number of sts)
Moss Stitch is worked flat, but which rows are RS and which are WS depend on the size vest being made.
Row 1: (K1, P1) to end.
Row 2: Rep Row 1.
Row 3: (P1, K1) to end.
Row 4: Rep Row 3.
Rep Rows 1-4 for pattern.
When working over an odd number of sts, end Rows 1 & 2 with K1 and Rows 3 & 4 with P1.

Diamond Cable (flat over a multiple of 36 sts plus 12)
Horizontal pattern reps are designated by asterisks *.
Rep between * and * 3 (3, 3, 3, 3, 5, 5, 5) times.
Setup Row 1 (RS): *2/2 LPC, K4, 2/2 RPC, (2/2 LPC, P4, 2/2 RC) two times*, 2/2 LPC, K4, 2/2 RPC.
Row 2 (WS): *K2, P8, (K4, P2) four times, K2*, K2, P8, K2.
Row 3: *P2, (2/2 RC) two times, (P4, 2/2 LPC, 2/2 RPC) two times, P2*, P2, (2/2 RC) two times, P2.
Row 4: *K2, P8, K2, (K4, P4, K4) two times*, K2, P8, K2.
Row 5: *P2, K2, 2/2 LC, K2, (P6, 2/2 RC) two times, P4*, P2, K2, 2/2 LC, K2, P2.
Row 6: Rep Row 4.
Row 7: *P2, (2/2 RC) two times, (P4, 2/2 RPC, 2/2 LPC) two times, P2*, P2, (2/2 RC) two times, P2.
Row 8: Rep Row 2.
Row 9: *P2, K2, 2/2 LC, K2, P2, (2/2 RPC, P4, 2/2 LPC) two times*, P2, K2, 2/2 LC, K2, P2.
Row 10: *K2, P8, K2, (P2, K8, P2) two times*, K2, P8, K2.
Row 11: *P2, (2/2 RC) two times, P2, K2, P8, 2/2 LC, P8, K2*, P2, (2/2 RC) two times, P2.
Row 12: Rep Row 10.
Row 13: *P2, K2, 2/2 LC, K2, P2, (2/2 LPC, P4, 2/2 RPC) two times*, P2, K2, 2/2 LC, K2, P2.
Rows 14-25: Rep Rows 2-13.
Rows 26-32: Rep Rows 2-8.
Row 33: *2/2 RPC, 2/2 LC, 2/2 LPC, (2/2 RPC, P4, 2/2 LPC) two times*, 2/2 RPC, 2/2 LC, 2/2 LPC.
Row 34: *P2, K2, P4, K2, (P4, K8) two times*, P4, K2, P4, K2, P2.
Row 35: K2, *P2, K4, P2, (2/2 LC, P8) two times, 2/2 LC*, P2, K4, P2, K2.
Row 36: Rep Row 34.
Row 37: *2/2 LPC, 2/2 RC, 2/2 RPC, (2/2 LPC, P4, 2/2 RC) two times*, 2/2 LPC, 2/2 RC, 2/2 RPC.
Rep Rows 2-37 for pattern.

Collar Transition (in the round over 40 sts)
Rnd 1: K6, (P4, K2) five times, K4.
Rnd 2: K4, (2/2 LPC, 2/2 RPC, P4) two times, 2/2 LPC, 2/2 RPC, K4.

Cable Rib—Round (in the round over a multiple of 6 sts)
Rnd 1: (P1, K4, P1) to end.
Rnd 2: Rep Rnd 1.
Rnd 3: (P1, 2/2 LC, P1) to end.
Rnds 4-6: Rep Rnd 1.
Rnd 7: (P1, 2/2 LDC, P1) to end. 1 st dec per rep.

DIRECTIONS

Back
Ribbing
CO 107 (117, 127, 137, 147, 157, 177, 187, 197) sts using Cabled Cast On.
Work Rows 1-7 of Cable Rib—Flat. 128 (140, 152, 164, 176, 188, 212, 224, 236) sts.
Rep Rows 4-7 of Cable Rib—Flat two more times.

Next Row (WS): Sl1, (K1, P1, P2tog, P1, K1) 0 (1, 2, 3, 4, 5, 1, 2, 3) times, (K1, P4, K1) 21 (21, 21, 21, 21, 21, 33, 33, 33) times, (K1, P1, P2tog, P1, K1) 0 (1, 2, 3, 4, 5, 1, 2, 3) times, K1. 128 (138, 148, 158, 168, 178, 210, 220, 230) sts.

Body

Setup Row (RS): Sl1, work Moss Stitch beginning with Row 2 (1, 2, 1, 2, 1, 1, 2, 1) over 3 (8, 13, 18, 23, 28, 8, 13, 18) sts, work Row 1 (Setup Row) of Diamond Cable across next 120 (120, 120, 120, 120, 120, 192, 192, 192) sts, repeating Sts 1-36 (if following chart) or between * and * (if following written instructions) 3 (3, 3, 3, 3, 3, 5, 5, 5) times before working final 12 Diamond Cable sts, then work Moss Stitch beginning with Row 2 (1, 2, 1, 2, 1, 1, 2, 1) over 3 (8, 13, 18, 23, 28, 8, 13, 18) sts, K1.

Cont as established until all rows of Diamond Cable have been worked, and then rep Rows 2-37 as necessary. Work until Back measures 13.75 (13.75, 14, 14, 14, 13.75, 14.5, 14.5, 15)" from CO edge, ending with a WS row.

Armholes

Note: Cont to follow Diamond Cable as far as possible while following dec instructions at the same time.

At beginning of next two rows, BO 5 (9, 9, 10, 11, 10, 10, 9, 9) sts, then work as established to end of row. 118 (120, 130, 138, 146, 158, 190, 202, 212) sts.

Next Row (RS): BO 3 sts, work as established to end.

Next Row (WS): BO 3 sts, work as established for 0 (0, 0, 0, 0, 0, 0, 2, 7) sts, (P2tog, P1) 2 (3, 2, 0, 0, 0, 2, 3, 2) times, work as established to last 7 (10, 1, 1, 1, 1, 7, 12, 14) sts, (P2tog, P1) 2 (3, 2, 0, 0, 0, 2, 3, 2) times, work as established for 0 (0, 0, 0, 0, 0, 0, 2, 7) sts, P1. 108 (108, 120, 132, 140, 152, 180, 190, 202) sts.

Dec 1 st at each edge on next row and 0 (0, 2, 2, 2, 2, 6, 4, 4) following rows, then on 3 (3, 2, 3, 3, 3, 3, 4, 5) following RS rows. 100 (100, 110, 120, 128, 140, 160, 172, 182) sts.

WE until Back measures 22.25 (22.25, 23.75, 23.75, 23.75, 23.75, 25.5, 25.5, 27)" from CO edge, ending with RS Row 7 (7, 19, 19, 19, 19, 31, 31, 7) of Diamond Cable; if row gauge differs from that listed, end with one of the following rows: Row 7, 19, or 31.

Back Left

Next Row (WS): Work as established over 30 (30, 35, 40, 44, 50, 60, 66, 71) sts. Place remaining sts on st holder or scrap yarn. Turn.

Next Row (RS): BO 3 (3, 3, 3, 3, 9, 9, 9, 9) sts. Work as established to end. 27 (27, 32, 37, 41, 41, 51, 57, 62) sts.

Next Row: Work as established to last st, P1.

Next Row: Sl1, P2tog, work as established to end. 1 st dec. Rep these two rows four more times. 22 (22, 27, 32, 36, 36, 46, 52, 57) sts.

WE for two rows as established, ending with RS Row 21 (21, 33, 33, 33, 33, 9, 9, 21) of Diamond Cable; if row gauge differs from that listed, end here with one of the following rows: Row 3, 9, 15, 21, 27, or 33. Note ending row number. BO all sts in rib.

Back Right

Return 30 (30, 35, 40, 44, 50, 60, 66, 71) sts from right edge to needles, leaving 40 sts on st holder for Back Neck. With WS facing, join yarn at neck edge and work as established to end.

Work one RS row as established.

Next Row (WS): BO 3 (3, 3, 3, 3, 9, 9, 9, 9) sts. Work as established to end. 27 (27, 32, 37, 41, 41, 51, 57, 62) sts.

Next Row: Work as established to last 3 sts, P2tog, K1. 1 st dec.

Next Row: Sl1, work as established to end. Rep these two rows four more times. 22 (22, 27, 32, 36, 36, 46, 52, 57) sts.

WE for one row as established, ending with RS Row 21 (21, 33, 33, 33, 33, 9, 9, 21) of Diamond Cable; if row gauge differs from that listed, end here with one of the following rows: Row 3, 9, 15, 21, 27, or 33. Note ending row number. BO all sts in rib.

Front

Follow instructions for Back through shaping for Armholes. 100 (100, 110, 120, 128, 140, 160, 172, 182) sts.

A 33.75 (37.25, 41, 44.5, 48.25, 51.75, 56.5, 60.25, 63.75)"
B 13.75 (13.75, 14, 14, 14, 13.75, 14.5, 14.5, 15)"
C 9.5 (9.5, 10.75, 10.75, 10.75, 11, 12, 12, 13)"
D 15 (15, 16, 17.75, 19, 21, 23, 24.75, 26)"
E 5.5 (5.5, 5.5, 5.5, 5.5, 7, 7, 7, 7)"
F 2.5" (front neck drop)
G 1" (back neck drop)

WE until Front measures 20.75 (20.75, 22.25, 22.25, 22.25, 23.75, 23.75, 25.5)" from CO edge, ending with RS Row 31 (31, 7, 7, 7, 7, 19, 19, 31) of Diamond Cable; if row gauge differs from that listed, end with one of the following rows: Row 7, 19, or 31.

Front Right
Next Row (WS): Work as established over 30 (30, 35, 40, 44, 50, 60, 66, 71) sts. Place remaining sts on st holder or scrap yarn. Turn.
Next Row (RS): BO 2 (2, 2, 2, 2, 6, 6, 6, 6) sts. Work as established to end. 28 (28, 33, 38, 42, 44, 54, 60, 65) sts.

Next Row (WS): Work as established to last st, P1.
Next Row: Sl1, P2tog, work as established to end. 1 st dec.
Rep these two rows 5 (5, 5, 5, 5, 7, 7, 7, 7) more times. 22 (22, 27, 32, 36, 36, 46, 52, 57) sts.
WE for 14 (14, 14, 14, 14, 10, 10, 10, 10) rows as established, ending with RS Row 23 (23, 35, 35, 35, 35, 11, 11, 23) of Diamond Cable; if row gauge differs from that listed, end here with one of the following rows: Row 5, 11, 17, 23, 29, or 35 (two rows beyond noted row number for Back Right/Left).
BO all sts in rib.

Front Left
Return 30 (30, 35, 40, 44, 50, 60, 66, 71) sts from right edge to needles, leaving 40 sts on st holder for Front Neck. With WS facing, join yarn at neck edge and work as established to end.
Work one row as established.
Next Row (WS): BO 2 (2, 2, 2, 2, 6, 6, 6, 6) sts. Work as established to end. (28, 33, 38, 42, 44, 54, 60, 65) sts.

Next Row (RS): Work as established to last 3 sts, P2tog, K1. 1 st dec.
Next Row: Sl1, work as established to end.
Rep these two rows 5 (5, 5, 5, 5, 7, 7, 7, 7) more times. 22 (22, 27, 32, 36, 36, 46, 52, 57) sts.

WE for 13 (13, 13, 13, 13, 9, 9, 9, 9) rows as established, ending with RS Row 23 (23, 35, 35, 35, 35, 11, 11, 23) of Diamond Cable; if row gauge differs from that listed, end here with one of the following rows: Row 5, 11, 17, 23, 29, or 35 (two rows beyond noted row number for Back Right/Left).
BO all sts in rib.

Seaming
Sew side seams using Mattress Stitch. Sew shoulder seams, matching up cables between Front and Back.

Neck Edging
Return live sts from Back and Front Neck to needles. Using needles for knitting in the rnd, with RS facing and starting with live sts from Back Neck, *work Rnd 1 of Collar Transition over 40 sts, PU and K 6 sts per 1" along left neck edge adjusting as necessary to end up with a multiple of 6 sts plus 2 sts, PM; rep from * once more.
Next Rnd: *Work Rnd 2 of Collar Transition over 40 sts, P1, work Rnd 1 of Cable Rib—Round to last st before next M, P1, SM; rep from * once more.
Next Rnd: 2/2 LC, P1, work Rnd 2 of Cable Rib—Round around to last 1 st, removing Ms; this is the new BOR.
Next 5 Rnds: Work Cable Rib—Round over all sts through Rnd 7.
BO all sts in Rib as established.

Armhole Edging (make two the same)
Using needles for knitting in the rnd, with RS facing, starting from underarm seam, PU and K 6 sts per 1" around armhole, adjusting as necessary to end up with a multiple of 6 sts. Work Rnds 1-7 of Cable Rib—Round.
BO all sts in Rib as established.

Finishing
Weave in ends, wash, and block to diagram.

LEGEND

- **No Stitch** — Placeholder—no stitch made
- **K** — RS: Knit stitch; WS: Purl stitch
- **P** — RS: Purl stitch; WS: Knit stitch
- **Sl** — RS: Slip stitch purl-wise, with yarn in back; WS: Slip stitch purl-wise, with yarn in front
- **Cable 2 Over 2 Right (2/2 RC)** — Sl2 to CN, hold in back; K2, K2 from CN
- **Cable 2 Over 2 Left (2/2 LC)** — Sl2 to CN, hold in front; K2, K2 from CN
- **Cable 2 Over 2 Right, Purl back (2/2 RPC)** — Sl2 to CN, hold in back; K2, P2 from CN
- **Cable 2 Over 2 Left, Purl back (2/2 LPC)** — Sl2 to CN, hold in front; P2, K2 from CN
- **Cable 2 Over 2 Left, Decrease back (2/2 LDC)** — Sl2 to CN, hold in front; K2tog, K2 from CN
- **Cable 2 Over 1 Left, Increase back (2/1 LIC)** — Sl2 to CN, hold in front; knit into front and back of stitch, K2 from CN
- **Pattern Repeat**

Cable Rib—Round

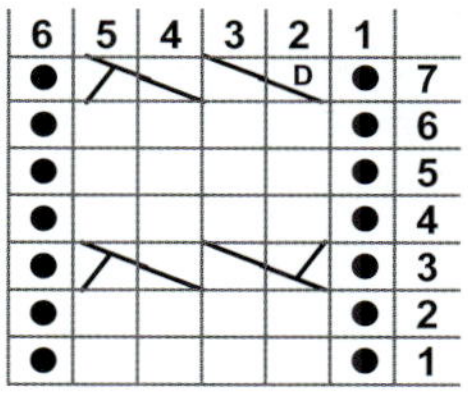

Cable Rib—Flat

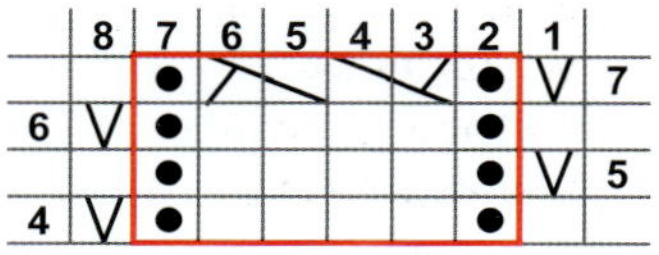

Setup Rows:

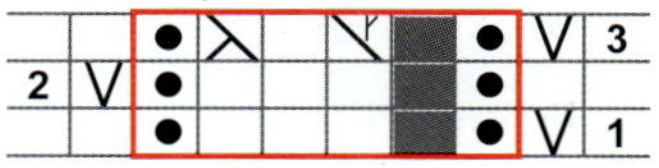

Collar Transition

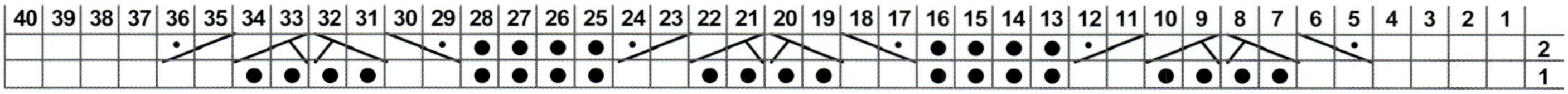

Diamond Cable

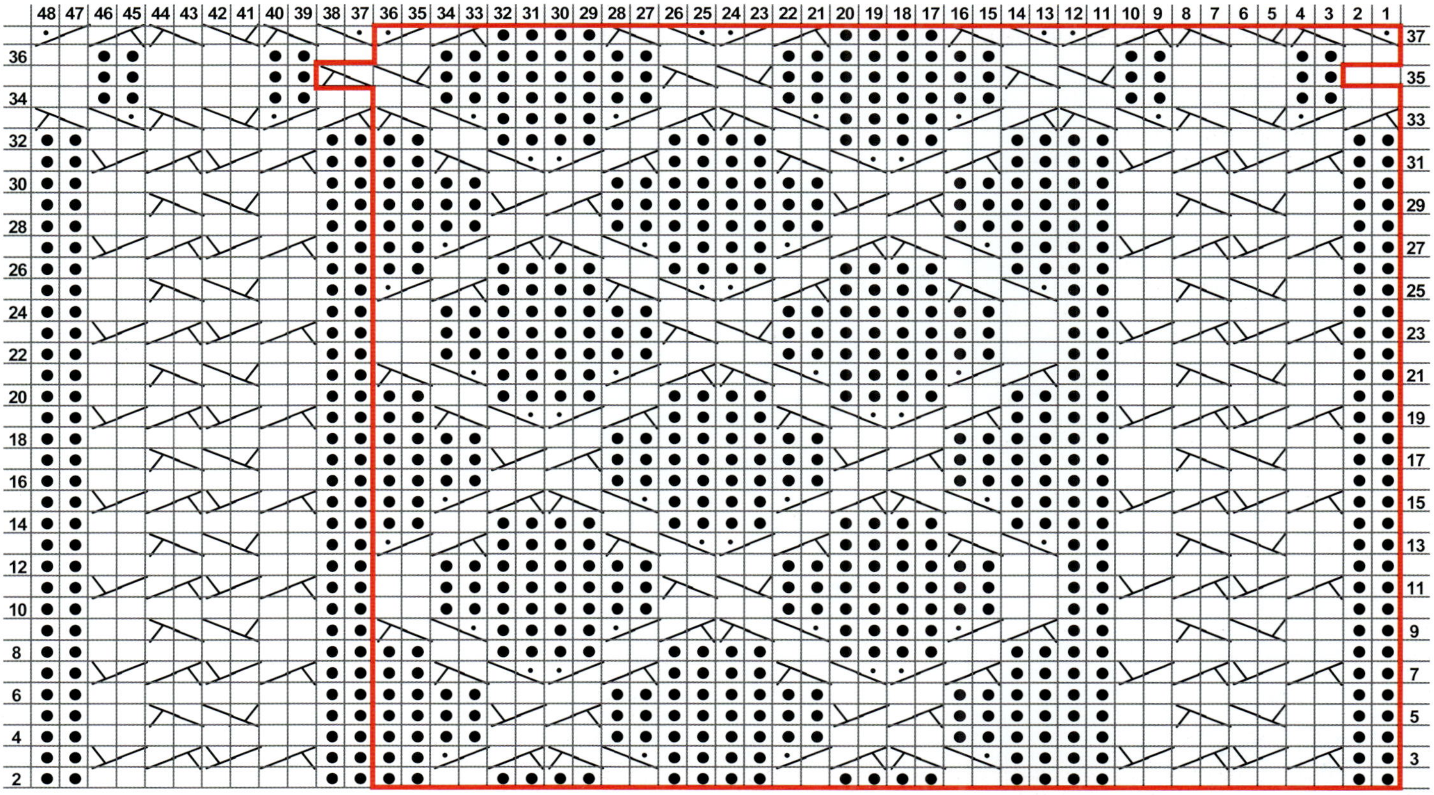

Setup Row:

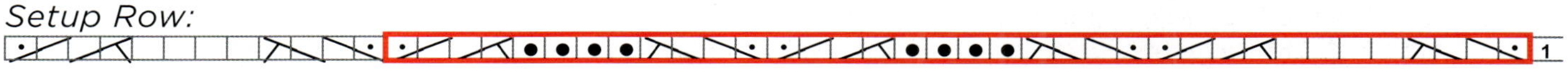

Sennit Vest

SONJA'S HAT

by Hope Vickman

FINISHED MEASUREMENTS
18 (20, 22)" circumference × 7.25 (8, 8.75)" height
Sample is 20" size

YARN
Palette™ (fingering weight, 100% Peruvian Highland Wool; 231 yards/50g): Rooibos Heather 25551, 2 balls

NEEDLES
US 1 (2.5mm) 16" circular needles, and DPNs or two 24" circular needles for two circulars technique or 32" or longer circular needles for Magic Loop technique, or size to obtain gauge

US 0 (2mm) 16" circular needles, or one size smaller than size used to obtain gauge

NOTIONS
Yarn Needle
8 (9, 10) Stitch Markers
1 Unique Stitch Marker
Cable Needle

GAUGE
44 sts and 42 rows = 4" in Cabled Stitch Pattern in the round, blocked

For pattern support, contact hopehafs@hotmail.com

Sonja's Hat

Notes:
Cascading cables create a beautiful allover texture that adds a Celtic charm and keeps the knitting engaging.

This hat is knit in the round from the bottom up. Decreases at the crown are cleverly hidden within the cables.

The charts are worked in the round; read each chart row from right to left as a RS row.

M1P (make 1 purl stitch)
Inserting LH needle from back to front, PU horizontal strand between st just worked and next st, and P into it.

2/2 LPC (cable 2 over 2 left, purl back)
Sl2 to CN, hold in front; P2, K2 from CN.

2/2 RPC (cable 2 over 2 right, purl back)
Sl2 to CN, hold in back; K2, P2 from CN.

2/2 LC (cable 2 over 2 left)
Sl2 to CN, hold in front; K2, K2 from CN.

2/2 RC (cable 2 over 2 right)
Sl2 to CN, hold in back; K2, K2 from CN.

2/2 LPDC (cable 2 over 2 left, purl decrease back)
Sl2 to CN, hold in front; P2tog, K2 from CN. 1 st dec.

2/2 RPDC (cable 2 over 2 right, purl decrease back)
Sl2 to CN, hold in back; K2, P2tog from CN. 1 st dec.

2/2 LDC (cable 2 over 2 left, decrease back)
Sl2 to CN, hold in front; K2tog, K2 from CN. 1 st dec.

2/2 RCSSK (cable 2 over 2 right, SSK back after cable)
Sl2 to CN, hold in back; K2, K1 from CN, SSK over next st from CN and next st from LH needle. 1 st dec.

2/2 RDC (cable 2 over 2 right, decrease back)
Sl2 to CN, hold in back; K2, K2tog from CN. 1 st dec.

1/2 LDC (cable 2 over 2 left, decrease back)
Sl1 to CN, hold in front; K2tog, K1 from CN. 1 st dec.

1/2 RDC (cable 2 over 2 right, decrease back)
Sl2 to CN, hold in back; K1, K2tog from CN. 1 st dec.

Cabled Stitch Pattern (in the round over a multiple of 22 sts after Setup Rnd)
Setup Rnd: (M1P, K2, P1, M1P, P2, K1, M1R, K2, M1P, K2, M1R, K1, P2, M1P, P1, K2) to end.
Rnd 1: (P1, K2, P4, K4, P1, K4, P4, K2) to end.
Rnd 2: (P1, 2/2 LPC, P2, K4, P1, K4, P2, 2/2 RPC) to end.
Rnd 3: (P3, K2, P2, K4, P1, K4, P2, K2, P2) to end.
Rnd 4: (P3, 2/2 LC, 2/2 LC, P1, 2/2 RC, 2/2 RC, P2) to end.
Rnd 5: (P3, K8, P1, K8, P2) to end.
Rnd 6: (P1, 2/2 RPC, 2/2 LPC, K2, P1, K2, 2/2 RPC, 2/2 LPC) to end.
Rnd 7: Rep Rnd 1.
Rnd 8: (P1, K2, P4, 2/2 LC, P1, 2/2 RC, P4, K2) to end.
Rep Rnds 1-8 for pattern.

DIRECTIONS

Ribbed Brim
Using smaller needles, loosely CO 144 (160, 176) sts. Place unique M for BOR, join to work in the rnd, being careful not to twist sts.
Work 1x1 Rib for 1.5".

Body
Next Rnd: Switch to larger needles. Working either from charted or written instructions, rep Setup Rnd of Cabled Stitch Pattern 9 (10, 11) times around, PM after each rep, keeping unique M in place for BOR. 198 (220, 242) sts.

Cont as established, SMs as reached, until all rnds of Cabled Stitch Pattern have been worked.
Rep Rnds 1-8 of charted or written Cabled Stitch Pattern instructions until hat measures 5.25 (6, 6.75)" from CO edge, ending with Rnd 8 of Cabled Stitch Pattern.

Crown Decreases
Work from written instructions below, or from chart. Each rep will be worked 9 (10, 11) times around. SMs as reached.

Rnd 1: (P1, K2, P4, K4, P1, K4, P4, K2) to end.
Rnd 2: (P1, 2/2 LPDC, P2, K4, P1, K4, P2, 2/2 RPDC) to end. 180 (200, 220) sts.
Rnd 3: (P2, K2, P2, K4, P1, K4, P2, K2, P1) to end.
Rnd 4: (P2, 2/2 LPDC, 2/2 LC, P1, 2/2 RC, 2/2 RPDC, P1) to end. 162 (180, 198) sts.
Rnd 5: (P3, K6, P1, K6, P2) to end.
Rnd 6: (P3, 2/2 LPDC, K2, P1, K2, 2/2 RPDC, P2) to end. 144 (160, 176) sts.
Rnd 7: (P4, K4, P1, K4, P3) to end.
Rnd 8: (P2, P2tog, 2/2 LC, P1, 2/2 RC, P2tog, P1) to end. 126 (140, 154) sts.
Rnd 9: (P3, K4, P1, K4, P2) to end.
Rnd 10: (P1, P2tog, K4, P1, K4, P2tog) to end. 108 (120, 132) sts.
Rnd 11: (P2, K4, P1, K4, P1) to end.
Rnd 12: (P2tog, 2/2 LC, P1, 2/2 RCSSK) to end. 90 (100, 110) sts.
Rnd 13: (P1, K4) to end.
Rnd 14: (K2tog, K3) to end. 72 (80, 88) sts.
Rnd 15: K all.
Rnd 16: (2/2 LDC, 2/2 RDC) to end. 54 (60, 66) sts.
Rnd 17: K all.
Rnd 18: (1/2 LDC, 1/2 RDC) to end. 36 (40, 44) sts.
Rnd 19: K all.
Rnd 20: (SSK, K2tog) to end. 18 (20, 22) sts.
Rnd 21: (SSK) to end, removing Ms. 9 (10, 11) sts.

Break yarn, thread tail through remaining sts, and cinch tight.

Finishing
Weave in ends, wash, and block to diagram.

LEGEND

■ **No Stitch** — Placeholder—no stitch made

☐ **Knit Stitch**

• **Purl Stitch**

╱ **K2tog** — Knit 2 stitches together as one stitch

╲ **SSK** — Slip, slip, knit slipped stitches together

╱ **P2tog** — Purl 2 stitches together as one stitch

MR **M1R** — Make 1 right-leaning stitch

MP **M1P** — Make 1 purl stitch

Cable 2 Over 2 Right (2/2 RC) — Sl2 to CN, hold in back; K2, K2 from CN

Cable 2 Over 2 Left (2/2 LC) — Sl2 to CN, hold in front; K2, K2 from CN

Cable 2 Over 2 Right, Purl back (2/2 RPC) — Sl2 to CN, hold in back; K2, P2 from CN

Cable 2 Over 2 Left, Purl back (2/2 LPC) — Sl2 to CN, hold in front; P2, K2 from CN

Cable 2 Over 2 Right, Decrease back (2/2 RDC) — Sl2 to CN, hold in back; K2, K2tog from CN

Cable 2 Over 2 Left, Decrease back (2/2 LDC) — Sl2 to CN, hold in front; K2tog, K2 from CN

Cable 1 Over 2 Right, Decrease back (1/2 RDC) — Sl2 to CN, hold in back; K1, K2tog from CN

Cable 1 Over 2 Left, Decrease back (1/2 LDC) — Sl1 to CN, hold in front; K2tog, K1 from CN

Cable 2 Over 2 Right, Purl Decrease back (2/2 RPDC) — Sl2 to CN, hold in back; K2, P2tog from CN

Cable 2 Over 2 Left, Purl Decrease back (2/2 LPDC) — Sl2 to CN, hold in front; P2tog, K2 from CN

Cable 2 Over 2 Right, SSK back after cable (2/2 RC-SSK) — Sl2 to CN, hold in back; K2, K1 from CN, then work SSK over next CN st and next st on left-hand needle

☐ **Pattern Repeat**

Cabled Stitch Pattern

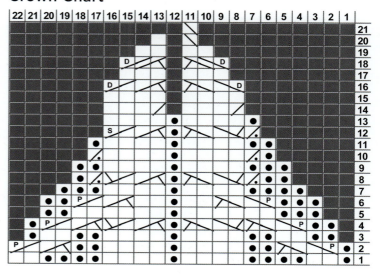

Crown Chart

Sonja's Hat

Glossary
Common Stitches & Techniques

Slipped Stitches (Sl)
Always slip stitches purl-wise with yarn held to the wrong side of work, unless noted otherwise in the pattern.

Make 1 Left-Leaning Stitch (M1L)
Inserting LH needle from front to back, PU the horizontal strand between the st just worked and the next st, and K TBL.

Make 1 Right-Leaning Stitch (M1R)
Inserting LH needle from back to front, PU the horizontal strand between the st just worked and the next st, and K TFL.

Slip, Slip, Knit (SSK)
(Sl1 K-wise) twice; insert LH needle into front of these 2 sts and knit them together.

Centered Double Decrease (CDD)
Slip first and second sts together as if to work K2tog; K1; pass 2 slipped sts over the knit st.

Stockinette Stitch (St st, flat over any number of sts)
Row 1 (RS): Knit all sts.
Row 2 (WS): Purl all sts.
Rep Rows 1-2 for pattern.
St st in the round: Knit every rnd.

Garter Stitch (in the round over any number of sts)
Rnd 1: Purl all sts.
Rnd 2: Knit all sts.
Rep Rnds 1-2 for pattern.
Garter Stitch flat: Knit every row.
(One Garter ridge is comprised of two rows/rnds.)

1x1 Rib (flat or in the round, over an even number of sts)
Row/Rnd 1: (K1, P1) to end of row/rnd.
Rep Row/Rnd 1 for pattern.

2x2 Rib (flat over a multiple of 4 sts plus 2)
Row 1 (RS): K2, (P2, K2) to end of row.
Row 2 (WS): P2, (K2, P2) to end of row.
Rep Rows 1-2 for pattern.

2x2 Rib (in the round over a multiple of 4 sts)
Rnd 1: (K2, P2) to end of rnd.
Rep Rnd 1 for pattern.

Magic Loop Technique
A technique using one long circular needle to knit in the round around a small circumference. A tutorial can be found at https://tutorials.knitpicks.com/wptutorials/magic-loop.

Knitting in the Round with Two Circular Needles
A technique using two long circulars to knit around a small circumference. A tutorial can be found at https://tutorials.knitpicks.com/knitting-in-the-round-with-2-circular-needles.

Backward Loop Cast On
A simple, all-purpose cast on that can be worked mid-row. Also called Loop, Single, or E-Wrap Cast On. A tutorial can be found at https://tutorials.knitpicks.com/loop-cast-on.

Long Tail Cast On
Fast and neat once you get the hang of it. Also referred to as the Slingshot Cast On. A tutorial can be found at https://tutorials.knitpicks.com/long-tail-cast-on.

Cabled Cast On
A strong and nice looking basic cast on that can be worked mid-project. A tutorial can be found at https://tutorials.knitpicks.com/cabled-cast-on.

3-Needle Bind Off
Used to easily seam two rows of live stitches together. A tutorial can be found at https://tutorials.knitpicks.com/3-needle-bind-off.

Abbreviations

approx	approximately	KFB	knit into front and back of stitch	PSSO	pass slipped stitch over	SSP	slip, slip, purl these 2 stitches together through back loop
BO	bind off	K-wise	knit-wise	PU	pick up	SSSK	slip, slip, slip, knit these 3 stitches together (like SSK)
BOR	beginning of round	LH	left hand	P-wise	purl-wise		
CN	cable needle	M	marker	rep	repeat		
C (1, 2…)	color (1, 2…)	M1	make 1 stitch	Rev St st	reverse stockinette stitch	St st	stockinette stitch (*see above*)
CC	contrast color	M1L	make 1 left-leaning stitch (*see above*)	RH	right hand	st(s)	stitch(es)
CDD	centered double decrease (*see above*)	M1R	make 1 right-leaning stitch (*see above*)	rnd(s)	round(s)	TBL	through back loop
CO	cast on			RS	right side	TFL	through front loop
cont	continue	MC	main color	Sk	skip	tog	together
dec(s)	decrease(es)	P	purl	SK2P	slip 1, knit 2 together, pass slipped stitch over	W&T	wrap & turn (for short rows; see next pg)
DPN(s)	double pointed needle(s)	P2tog	purl 2 stitches together				
inc(s)	increase(s)	P3tog	purl 3 stitches together	SKP	slip, knit, pass slipped stitch over	WE	work even
K	knit			Sl	slip (*see above*)	WS	wrong side
K2tog	knit 2 stitches together	PM	place marker	SM	slip marker	WYIB	with yarn in back
K3tog	knit 3 stitches together	PFB	purl into front and back of stitch	SSK	slip, slip, knit these 2 stitches together (*see above*)	WYIF	with yarn in front
						YO	yarn over

Cabling Without a Cable Needle
Tutorials for 1 over 1 cables can be found at https://blog.knitpicks.com/tutorial-1-over-1-cables-without-a-cable-needle. A tutorial for standard cables can be found at https://tutorials.knitpicks.com/learn-to-cable-without-a-cable-needle.

Felted Join (to splice yarn)
One method for joining a new length of yarn to the end of one that is already being used. A tutorial can be found at https://tutorials.knitpicks.com/felted-join.

Mattress Stitch
A neat, invisible seaming method that uses the bars between the first and second stitches on the edges. A tutorial can be found at https://tutorials.knitpicks.com/mattress-stitch.

Provisional Cast On (crochet method)
Used to cast on stitches that are also a row of live stitches, so they can be put onto a needle and used later.
Directions: Using a crochet hook, make a slipknot, then hold knitting needle in left hand, hook in right. With yarn in back of needle, work a chain st by pulling yarn over needle and through chain st. Move yarn back to behind needle, and rep for the number of sts required. Chain a few more sts off the needle, then break yarn and pull end through last chain. (CO sts may be incorrectly mounted; if so, work into backs of these sts.) To unravel later (when sts need to be picked up), pull chain end out; chain should unravel, leaving live sts. A video tutorial can be found at https://tutorials.knitpicks.com/crocheted-provisional-cast-on.

Provisional Cast On (crochet chain method)
Same result as the crochet method above, but worked differently, so you may prefer one or the other.
Directions: With a crochet hook, use scrap yarn to make a slipknot and chain the number of sts to be cast on, plus a few extra sts. Insert tip of knitting needle into first bump of crochet chain. Wrap project yarn around needle as if to knit, and pull yarn through crochet chain, forming first st. Rep this process until you have cast on the correct number of sts. To unravel later (when sts need to be picked up), pull chain out, leaving live sts. A photo tutorial can be found at https://tutorials.knitpicks.com/crocheted-provisional-cast-on.

Judy's Magic Cast On
This method creates stitches coming out in opposite directions from a seamless center line, perfect for starting toe-up socks.
Directions: Make a slipknot and place loop around one of the two needles; anchor loop counts as first st. Hold needles tog, with needle that yarn is attached to on top. In other hand, hold yarn so tail goes over index finger and yarn attached to ball goes over thumb. Bring tip of bottom needle over strand of yarn on finger (top strand), around and under yarn and back up, making a loop around needle. Pull loop snug. Bring top needle (with slipknot) over yarn tail on thumb (bottom strand), around and under yarn and back up, making a loop around needle. Pull loop snug. Cont casting on sts until desired number is reached; top yarn strand always wraps around bottom needle, and bottom yarn strand always wraps around top needle. A tutorial can be found at https://tutorials.knitpicks.com/judys-magic-cast-on.

Stretchy Bind Off
Directions: K2, *insert LH needle into front of 2 sts on RH needle and knit them tog—1 st remains on RH needle. K1; rep from * until all sts have been bound off. A tutorial can be found at https://tutorials.knitpicks.com/go-your-own-way-socks-toe-up-part-7-binding-off.

Jeny's Surprisingly Stretchy Bind Off (for 1x1 Rib)
Directions: Reverse YO, K1, pass YO over; *YO, P1, pass YO and previous st over P1; reverse YO, K1, pass YO and previous st over K1; rep from * until 1 st is left, then break working yarn and pull it through final st to complete BO.

Kitchener Stitch (also called Grafting)
Seamlessly join two sets of live stitches together.
Directions: With an equal number of sts on two needles, break yarn leaving a tail approx four times as long as the row of sts, and thread through a blunt yarn needle. Hold needles parallel with WSs facing in and both needles pointing to the right. Perform Step 2 on the first front st, then Step 4 on the first back st, then continue from Step 1, always pulling yarn tightly so the grafted row tension matches the knitted fabric:
Step 1: Pull yarn needle K-wise through front st and drop st from knitting needle.
Step 2: Pull yarn needle P-wise through next front st, leaving st on knitting needle.
Step 3: Pull yarn needle P-wise through first back st and drop st from knitting needle.
Step 4: Pull yarn needle K-wise through next back st, leaving st on knitting needle.
Rep Steps 1-4 until all sts have been grafted together, finishing by working Step 1 through the last remaining front st, then Step 3 through the last remaining back st. Photo tutorials can be found at https://blog.knitpicks.com/tutorial-grafting-with-kitchener-stitch-stockinette-garter.

Short Rows
There are several options for how to handle short rows, so you may see different suggestions/intructions in a pattern.

Wrap and Turn (W&T) (one option for Short Rows)
Work until the st to be wrapped. If knitting: Bring yarn to front, Sl next st P-wise, return yarn to back; turn work, and Sl wrapped st onto RH needle. Cont across row. If purling: Bring yarn to back of work, Sl next st P-wise, return yarn to front; turn work and Sl wrapped st onto RH needle. Cont across row.
Picking up Wraps: Work to wrapped st. If knitting: Insert RH needle under wrap, then through wrapped st K-wise; K st and wrap tog. If purling: Sl wrapped st P-wise onto RH needle, use LH needle to lift wrap and place it onto RH needle; Sl wrap and st back onto LH needle, and P tog.
A tutorial for W&T can be found at https://tutorials.knitpicks.com/short-rows-wrap-and-turn-or-wt.

German Short Rows (another option for Short Rows)
Work to turning point; turn. WYIF, Sl first st P-wise. Bring yarn over back of right needle, pulling firmly to create a "double stitch" on RH needle. If next st is a K st, leave yarn at back; if next st is a P st, bring yarn to front between needles. When it's time to work into double st, knit both strands tog.

THIS COLLECTION FEATURES

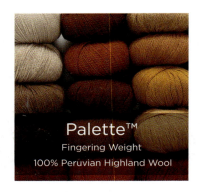

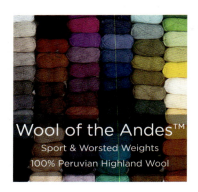
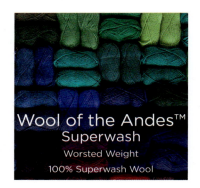

View these beautiful yarns and more at www.KnitPicks.com

Knit Picks yarn is both luxe and affordable—a seeming contradiction trounced! But it's not just about the pretty colors; we also care deeply about fiber quality and fair labor practices, leaving you with a gorgeously reliable product you'll turn to time and time again.